El Salvador

A Spring Whose Waters Never Run Dry

Edited by

Scott Wright
Minor Sinclair, EPICA
Margaret Lyle
David Scott

Foreword by
Jon Sobrino, S.J.

Ecumenical Program on Central America and the Caribbean (EPICA)
Christians for Peace in El Salvador (CRISPAZ)
Religious Task Force on Central America

Material originally published in Spanish in *Carta a las Iglesias* © *UCA Editores*

© 1990 by Ecumenical Program on Central America and the Caribbean (EPICA)
1470 Irving St. N.W., Washington, D.C.   20010. U.S.A.
Second Printing, 1990.

Cost: $6.00 plus $1.50 postage and handling.

Illustrations by Cerezo Barredo
Book and cover design: The Center for Educational Design and Communication,
                    Washington, D.C.

Library of Congress Cataloging in Publication Data
Wright, Scott; Sinclair, Minor; Lyle, Margaret; and Scott, David, Editors

El Salvador: A Spring Whose Waters Never Run Dry.

1. El Salvador–Politics–Human Rights–1980-1989
2. Catholic Church–El Salvador–Political Activity

ISBN 0-918346-09-6

For the 75,000 who have died

CONTENTS

Stories and testimonies of a people who die a slow death from poverty and are massacred by death squads and Army invasions.

Stories and testimonies of the people's determination to struggle for the cause of justice.

PART THREE: A CHURCH OF THE POOR 48-62

Stories and testimonies of the Christian base communities and their celebration of life and hope in the midst of violence and destruction.

PART FOUR: A NEW HEAVEN AND A NEW EARTH 62-74

Stories and testimonies of the witness of the Churches and their contribution to the struggle for liberation.

Stories and testimonies of a crucified people who witness to the power of resurrection in history.

FOREWORD

In El Salvador, 1990 is a year of anniversaries. The best known are the martyrdom of Archbishop Oscar Romero and the killing of four North American church-women: Ita Ford, Maura Clarke, Dorothy Kazel and Jean Donovan. Above all, 1990 culminates a decade of tragedy and hope for the Salvadoran people.

In November 1989 six of my brother Jesuits were murdered in El Salvador. I now understand better the indignation and outrage of thousands of Salvadorans whose family members have been killed. These Jesuits were men of hope, men of life, and they shared the destiny of the poor.

The poor in El Salvador, as in many Latin American countries, want to live, to have enough food to eat and land to work. But when they organize to obtain these rights that we take for granted, they are killed by the thousands. Salvadorans say that the wealthy countries ignore the great scandal that two-thirds of humankind is dying in poverty. This is because wealth and power can exist for the few only when the many suffer and die in poverty. The martyrs of El Salvador and of the world have been killed because they threatened the idols of wealth and power. My brother Jesuits defied these idols by telling the truth and unmasking lies. To tell the truth is to defy the idols of death.

What happens when, in El Salvador, we defy these idols of death? We become like the Suffering Servant of God. Isaiah presents the Suffering Servant as a mysterious person with a disfigured face. That is the reality of the Salvadoran people. When I look at the pictures of my brother Jesuits, I see that they also have been disfigured through torture and death. Isaiah says that the Suffering Servant is so disfigured that people who pass turn their heads away. It is nauseating to see this reality.

When we look face to face at the Suffering Servant, at the crucified People of God today, we must ask ourselves: how are we responsible for their suffering?

Archbishop Romero once said that he rejoiced that priests were being murdered in El Salvador. He went on to say that it would be very sad if, in a country where so many people are being assassinated, priests—as symbols of the Church—were not assassinated also. If priests are assassinated in El Salvador, it is because the Church has truly become Salvadoran. When the Church identifies so deeply with the poor that it suffers the same fate as the poor, then there is great love. This is an incarnation of God in our midst.

•••

The testimonies in this book are drawn from *Carta a las Iglesias* [Letter to the Churches], a publication of the University of Central America (UCA) in San Salvador. Each time I prepare a new issue of *Carta a las Iglesias*, I feel overwhelmed and moved. These testimonies always raise basic questions: How is it possible, Lord, that there is so much unjust suffering? Where do these people find the strength to live, to hope and to believe?

These stories testify to the people's hope and faith. They are an offering to the God of life in the midst of the idols of death. They have been given to us by the poor, by a crucified people who are "a light to the nations" (Isaiah 60:3) and "the wisdom of God" (Romans 1:24).

I see a light and salvation in the poor of this world which cannot be found elsewhere. That is why this book, *El Salvador: A Spring Whose Waters Never Run Dry*, is so valuable. It bears witness to what has happened during these past ten years in my country.

We should read this book with repentance for what we—in El Salvador and the United States—have contributed to this tragedy; and with gratitude for what the poor offer and teach us. Above all, we should read it with determination to defend the life and dignity of the poor.

My hope is that we will respond to these testimonies by raising our voices with those of the poor, offering them our solidarity when almost all the powers of the world—political, economic, military, cultural and even at times religious—are against them.

In this way we will become a little more human and a little more Christian.

Jon Sobrino, S.J.

January 1990
Oscar Romero Pastoral Center
University of Central America
San Salvador

El Salvador

Inset map:

CUBA
JAMAICA
CARIBBEAN SEA
COLOMBIA
PANAMA
NICARAGUA
HONDURAS
BELIZE
GUATEMALA
MEXICO
EL SALVADOR
PACIFIC OCEAN
0   400 kms

Main map:

HONDURAS

GUATEMALA

NICARAGUA

Gulf of Fonseca

Pacific Ocean

Departments and places:

MORAZAN
Perquin
San Francisco Gotera

LA UNION
La Union

SAN MIGUEL
San Miguel

USULUTAN
El Triunfo
Berlin
Usulutan

Cuco Beach

CABANAS
Sensuntepeque

SAN VICENTE
San Vicente

CHALATENANGO
La Palma
Arcatao
Chalatenango
Embalse Presa del Cerron Grande
El Paraiso
Aguilares
Suchitoto
RIO SUMPUL

CUSCATLAN
Cojutepeque

SAN SALVADOR
San Salvador
Nueva San Salvador

LA PAZ
Lake Ilopango
Santiago Nonualco
Comalapa

LA LIBERTAD
La Libertad

RIO LEMPA

SANTA ANA
Santa Ana

SONSONATE
Izalco
Sonsonate
Acajutla

AHUACHAPAN
Ahuachapan

KEY

- – – –   International boundary
- ········   Departmental boundaries
- ━━━━   Inter-American Highway
- ╱╱╱╱   Zones under guerrilla control. as of Autumn 1984

0 10 20 30 kms

INTRODUCTION

The Nahuatl Indians who first settled this mountainous land called it Cuscatlán, the Jewel by the Sea. When the Spaniards arrived in 1522 they renamed it El Salvador, Spanish for "the Saviour."

El Salvador. Many North Americans associate this land with violence, torture and death. An archbishop has been assassinated in El Salvador, nuns raped and 75,000 civilians have been killed in a ten-year reign of terror.

But for the Salvadoran people, particularly the poor, El Salvador also means a determined hope for a better life, no matter what the cost. El Salvador's poor are the most qualified to interpret their country's reality for us. They do so in this collection of testimonies, prayers, homilies and reflections.

• • •

The violence directed against El Salvador's poor has not been without purpose; the response of the poor not without reason.

Historically, the fundamental cause of injustice in El Salvador has been the extremely unequal distribution of land. One hundred years ago most of the land in El Salvador was owned and farmed communally. Under this system, life was hard but most people were self-sufficient. In the

1880s members of El Salvador's oligarchy passed laws to dispossess the indigenous people of their communal lands. They transformed these lands into large plantations and planted coffee, sugarcane and cotton as cash crops. When the people resisted efforts to seize their lands, or when the plantation workers organized to demand higher wages, they were killed.

In 1932—fifty years after the oligarchy seized the communal lands—Farabundo Martí led a peasant rebellion. The government responded by massacring 30,000 people. This event was called *la matanza*, the massacre. Scholars consider it the key to El Salvador's subsequent history. The oligarchy also outlawed indigenous culture; weaving traditional cloth was forbidden, as were the Nahuatl language and native music. For the next fifty years the poor in the countryside lived in virtual enslavement to the oligarchy under a succession of military dictatorships.

Following the Second Vatican Council (1962-1965) and the Latin American Bishops' Conference at Medellín, Colombia in 1968, social justice became a central concern for the Catholic Church. This "preferential option for the poor" ruptured the long-standing alliance between the Church and the oligarchy. The Church developed new approaches to evangelization and pastoral work. In areas such as the sugarcane-growing region around Aguilares, priests invited the *campesinos*—farmworkers and day laborers—to read and discuss Scripture in small groups. The people heard a Biblical message of justice and liberation and applied it to their lives. From these reflection groups, Christian base communities were born and grew.

Nuns and priests who supported efforts of the poor to organize became targets of the military's wrath. The first priest to be killed was Father Rutilio Grande of the parish of Aguilares, who was assassinated on March 12, 1977. Soon, the blood of other Christian martyrs would be shed as well.

The stark exploitation of the poor and the persecution of pastoral workers transformed the Church. Archbishop Oscar Romero, originally a conservative bishop, became increasingly critical of the government. He said, "It is not enough to undertake works of charity to alleviate the suffering of the poor; we must work to transform the structures that create this suffering."

As the Church continued to challenge the government and military, thousands more Christians, many of them catechists and delegates of the Word, were killed. Archbishop Romero himself was slain at the altar while celebrating Mass on March 24, 1980.

• • •

At the same time that these changes were taking place in the Church, social conditions continued to deteriorate during the 1970s. The poor responded by forming "popular organizations" to work for change. (In Spanish, *popular* means "of the people.") These included coalitions of trade unions, farmworker cooperatives, student groups and poor residents of marginalized neighborhoods. By early 1980 demonstrations with hundreds of thousands of participants were common. Members of these organizations filled the streets demanding justice. Opposition political leaders called for constitutional change and basic reforms, particularly land reform.

Once again, state repression was brutal. Union leaders, *campesinos*, teachers, churchworkers and others "were disappeared" by government death squads. Their mutilated bodies were often found lying by the roadside. Leaders of opposition parties were denounced as "communists" and gunned down. The Armed Forces fired on demonstrations, killing hundreds. Government repression decimated the popular organizations and ended virtually all expression of dissent.

Faced with extermination, thousands

from the popular organizations took up arms against the government, joining the guerrilla insurgency known as the Farabundo Martí National Liberation Front (FMLN). On January 10, 1981 the FMLN called for a nation-wide insurrection to bring about the social changes which the ruling class had denied for centuries. The FMLN gained control over large parts of the countryside, particularly the mountainous regions of northern Chalatenango and Morazán.

Since 1981, the United States has poured more than four billion dollars into El Salvador's counterinsurgency war. United States advisers have trained the Salvadoran military, and the U. S. Embassy in San Salvador largely directs the course of the war.

The single goal of this counterinsurgency strategy has been to prevent the FMLN from taking power. The targets, however, have mainly been suspected guerrilla supporters among the civilian population as well as FMLN combatants. The Salvadoran Army militarized the countryside, killing thousands of civilians.

Any act perceived as opposing the government was considered "subversive." Members of the Armed Forces and paramilitary organizations formed death squads. They set up a system of informants throughout the country and made lists of unionists, students, journalists and pastoral workers. By day and by night they dragged these people from their homes to torture and kill them.

Over the past ten years 75,000 civilians have been killed, most by the military and death squads. In the northern part of the country survivors of government massacres have fled to refugee camps in Honduras. Hundreds of thousands more have been displaced by government bombing in the countryside and have crowded into the poor neighborhoods of San Salvador.

The mid-1980s saw a renewal of popular organizing in the countryside, poor neighborhoods and workplaces. Hundreds of organizations united in a "popular movement" to demand structural change and a negotiated solution to the war. Refugees and displaced persons successfully overcame the military's opposition and returned to repopulate their homes in war zones.

When the ultra-right ARENA party gained control of the Salvadoran government in March 1989, the assault on the popular organizations intensified. "Disappearances," captures and killings increased dramatically after the election. On October 31, 1989 the office of a labor federation was bombed, killing ten people and wounding dozens.

Two weeks later the FMLN mounted a major offensive in the capital San Salvador. In retaliation, the government bombed poor neighborhoods and attacked the popular organizations. Many churchworkers, including foreigners, were imprisoned or forced to flee the country. During this offensive, members of the United States-trained Atlacatl Battalion invaded the University of Central America and slaughtered six Jesuit priests, their housekeeper and her daughter.

These killings and the thousands of human rights violations over the past ten years confirm Archbishop Romero's prediction to President Jimmy Carter in 1980. Romero wrote, "Instead of favoring greater justice and peace in El Salvador, your government's contribution will undoubtedly intensify the injustice and the repression." Romero's words have proven chillingly true. His plea to cut off aid to the Salvadoran military remains compellingly urgent.

• • •

El Salvador: A Spring Whose Waters Never Run Dry commemorates the tenth anniversary of the martyrdom of Archbishop Oscar Romero. Shortly before his death, Romero prophesied that if he were killed he would be resurrected in the Salvadoran people. We offer these selections as proof of that resurrection, revealed in the courage and perseverance of the Salvadoran people.

These testimonies, prayers and reflections come from Christian base communities, refugee camps, repopulated villages, poor urban neighborhoods and popular organizations. They were gathered by the Oscar Romero Pastoral Center of the University of Central America. Five of the Jesuits killed in November 1989 collaborated with Jon Sobrino and the staff at the Oscar Romero Pastoral Center to publish these testimonies in the newsletter, *Carta a las Iglesias*. Since 1986, selections from *Carta* have been translated into English and published as *Letter to the Churches*.

• • •

We wish to thank the Center for Educational Design and Communication, a project of the Religious of the Sacred Heart, for their excellent work on production. Mavi Coakley, RSCJ and Catherine Collins, RSCJ of the Center offered valuable advice and support. Melanie Guste, RSCJ designed *El Salvador: A Spring Whose Waters Never Run Dry*.

Lee Miller of the Religious Task Force on Central America and Hugo Bonilla provided valuable assistance in production of the book.

Father Jim Barnett, O.P. and the Rev. Bill Dexheimer, a Lutheran pastor, gave crucial support and encouragement to this project while serving as missionaries in El Salvador. Father Peter Hinde, O.Carm., the Rev. Dan Long of the Evangelical Lutheran Church in America, Betsy Ruth, Garth Cheff and Renny Golden contributed valuable advice and assistance. Christie Rodgers helped with promotion.

Margarita Studemeister, Catherine Sunshine, Chris Megargee and Maria Kaefer read several drafts of the manuscript and offered valuable comments.

In addition, the following organizations provided invaluable support to this project: the Carmelite Province of the Most Pure Heart of Mary, the Dominican Sisters of the Sick Poor, Sojourners Magazine, Dominican Sisters, Project El Salvador, the Ecumenical Program on Central America and the Caribbean (EPICA), Christians for Peace in El Salvador (CRISPAZ), and the Religious Task Force on Central America.

The Editors
January 1990

NOTHING IS AS IMPORTANT TO THE CHURCH AS HUMAN LIFE,
ESPECIALLY THE LIVES OF THE POOR AND THE OPPRESSED.

JESUS SAID THAT WHATEVER IS DONE TO THE POOR IS DONE TO HIM.

THIS BLOODSHED, THESE DEATHS, ARE BEYOND ALL POLITICS.
THEY TOUCH THE VERY HEART OF GOD.

ARCHBISHOP OSCAR ROMERO
MARCH 16, 1980

A TESTIMONY OF REPRESSION

ORIGINAL SIN

In the past ten years 75,000 Salvadorans have been killed. Most have been civilians murdered by government security forces or government-sponsored death squads. The purpose of the repression has not only been to kill leaders of opposition groups, but also to terrorize the population into submission.

The following testimony is one of thousands which speak of this horror.

"When night comes, I wish that I were a dove so I could fly far away and not have to be at home during these hours." So said Jacinta, a 50-year-old woman who fled the repression in the countryside and now lives with her family in a poor neighborhood of San Salvador. One night six men from a paramilitary organization came to her house "looking for guns."

"If I had guns, I would have sold them to buy food," she told them.

The men searched the family's shack. When they did not find anything they knocked down Jacinta's husband, stepped on him and kicked him, breaking his neck.

"God sees what you do," Jacinta cried out to them, "and God will make you pay for this shameful act."

"God is dead!" one of the men shouted. "We are the gods now." They then dragged Jacinta's two oldest daughters outside and raped them.

As they left, they threatened Jacinta, "If you tell anyone about this, we will come back and kill all of you."

Jacinta's five-year-old daughter—her youngest—witnessed everything that happened. Since then, the child hardly speaks. Jacinta's two daughters were left pregnant. Though Jacinta's husband survived, he is incapacitated. The family lives in fear.

Such incidents are common throughout El Salvador. Soldiers re-enact the original sin, believing they are "gods." *July 1981*

GOD SAW THAT HUMAN WICKEDNESS WAS GREAT ON EARTH AND THAT THE HUMAN HEART CONTRIVED NOTHING BUT WICKED SCHEMES ALL DAY LONG. GOD REGRETTED HAVING MADE HUMAN BEINGS ON EARTH AND WAS GRIEVED AT HEART.

GENESIS 6:5-6

THE TESTIMONY OF A MOTHER

DON'T TAKE MY CHILD AWAY!

In the mountainous regions of northern Chalatenango where FMLN guerrillas are active, the government Army has waged a murderous war against the poor. The objective of death squad assassinations, massacres of the civilian population and indiscriminate bombings has been to cut off popular support for the guerrillas. In this testimony a young mother tells of her community's forced flight, or guinda, *during an Army invasion.*

When the shooting began, we fled to the Sumpul River. Even though the river was flooded, I decided to jump in. As I neared the deepest part, I felt the current pulling my child away. I was terrified but we managed to get to the other side of the river.

We continued fleeing from the Army. At last we came to a hill and stopped to rest. We stayed there for three days until we saw soldiers coming toward us.

We began to run. They shouted, "Stop! Stop! We won't hurt you."

But we continued to flee. When they saw us escaping, they began to shoot. I fell and a soldier grabbed me. He threatened, "If you run, I'll kill you!" I stood and watched as soldiers captured many people, mostly mothers and children. They forced my mother to go with them. We were all taken to the woods.

A helicopter landed. The soldiers filled it with crying children and the helicopter flew away.

After a while the helicopter returned. The soldiers grabbed my child. I held him even more tightly. But they said, "We're taking this child!" and wrested him from my arms.

Hardly any adults were taken—only children. The soldiers said they were taking the children to San Martín and later, when they grew up, to the United States.

All this happened on a hill near the church in Manaquil, in the Department of Chalatenango, during the first days of June. My son was six months old; now he is eight months old. I am 17 years old. I want to ask Archbishop Rivera y Damas and the Human Rights Commission to do everything possible to return my child to me. I cry for him all the time, and I want desperately to see him again. *August 1982*

THEN WERE FULFILLED THE WORDS SPOKEN THROUGH THE PROPHET JEREMIAH, "A VOICE IS HEARD IN RAMAH, LAMENTING AND WEEPING BITTERLY: IT IS RACHEL WEEPING FOR HER CHILDREN, REFUSING TO BE COMFORTED BECAUSE THEY ARE NO MORE."
MATTHEW 2:17-18

The Testimony of a Refugee

EXODUS AT THE SUMPUL RIVER

The names of many places in El Salvador—the Lempa River, Las Hojas, Mozote—have a special meaning for the people because of the horrors committed there. One such place, the Sumpul River, was the site of two large Army massacres. The first occurred on May 14, 1980 when 600 men, women and children were killed as they tried to flee across the river to Honduras. Two years later, a second massacre took place, killing another 200 civilians.

Tonia, a survivor of the second massacre, gave this testimony in a refugee camp in Honduras. She appeared tired and in poor health. She had dark circles under her eyes. Like many of the children, women and elderly people in the camp, her feet were still soaked in blood. She held her baby in her arms, as her husband stood beside her.

It's not easy for me to talk—we've been walking for nine days and nights and I'm exhausted—but I'll try.

We were fleeing from the military and had gathered to cross the Sumpul River. There were about 5,000 of us, all civilians; no one was armed. Suddenly soldiers attacked us. They were about 300 yards away when they started firing.

We dropped everything we were carrying and ran. Children fell on top of each other, and adults stepped on children, because everybody panicked. The men cleared a path through the bushes so that people could escape.

We ran down the bank of the Sumpul River and into the water. Some of the children were swept downstream. Many elderly people couldn't resist the current and drowned. Some women who had been shot in the legs could not run and were left behind.

If God had not protected us, the whole community would have been killed. Yet in the midst of this terrible confusion, there was compassion. Some men helped mothers to get their children across the river. Parents who had lost their own children carried children that were not their own. The chaos was terrifying. There was crying and shooting on all sides. Many people drowned. Then, silence.

Those of us who made it to the other side of the river kept running, but the gunfire followed us. Finally we reached a hill and hid in the woods where we stayed for two days. The children cried from hunger. Some of them died because there was nothing to eat and their mothers had no milk. We couldn't find anything to eat. When the babies cried, we became scared that the Army would hear them and find us. Their mothers stuffed rags in the babies' mouths to stop the crying, but some of them suffocated to death. Others did not die right then, but the rags made their mouths so dry that they were unable to nurse. Other babies cried and cried, because their mothers were not there.

The following night we all left. The Army did not want us to escape. Their objective was to exterminate us so that not a single person would remain alive.

It was a miracle of God that we survived. God saved us in order to show the enemy that they are not all-powerful.

Fortunately, with God's help, we found the rest of our community. We joined them and escaped through a ravine. We cried and cried for all of those who had been killed. There was no food to eat. We ate raw corn, roots and leaves. We made soup out of grass and leaves. After that there

I remember what the people of Israel experienced when Pharaoh pursued them in order to exterminate them. We know their experience.

We spent the whole night running. We ran for hours, from hill to hill, from ravine to ravine. When dawn came, we were still running. The elderly people could not go any further. The mothers were exhausted and the children too tired to cry. We were dying of hunger and thirst. At first we had some green mangoes and cactus leaves but later we did not even have time to scavenge for food.

The enemy finally located us. They flew overhead in helicopters and shouted at us, "Guerrillas! We are the Belloso Battalion!"

They shot at us and dropped bombs and threw grenades. Bullets rained down on us from all sides. Many people were killed.

was nothing. Some of us had not eaten for nine days, others for twelve days. But thanks to the great power of God and the Holy Virgin who guided us, we are still alive.

I remember what the people of Israel experienced when Pharaoh pursued them in order to exterminate them. We know their experience. *July 1982*

THEN MOSES STRETCHED OUT HIS HAND OVER THE SEA, AND GOD DROVE THE SEA BACK WITH A STRONG EASTERLY WIND ALL NIGHT AND MADE THE SEA INTO DRY LAND. THE WATERS WERE DIVIDED AND THE ISRAELITES WENT ON DRY GROUND RIGHT THROUGH THE SEA, WITH WALLS OF WATER TO THE RIGHT AND LEFT OF THEM.
EXODUS 14:21B-22

MOZOTE: CRUCIFIXION OF THE SALVADORAN PEOPLE

More than 1,000 men, women and children were killed on December 12 and 13, 1981 in the massacre at Mozote, in the Department of Morazán. The massacre was committed by the Atlacatl Battalion, an elite Army unit trained in counterinsurgency by the U.S. government.

The following is the testimony of a 41-year-old woman, Rufina, the only witness to the massacre.

I believe I am the only survivor of the Mozote massacre. The village was filled with children because the people in the surrounding area had fled their homes to take refuge there. That is why the Army was able to kill so many people.

The soldiers from the Atlacatl Battalion came at seven in the morning. They said they had orders to kill everyone. Nobody was to remain alive. They locked the women in the houses and the men in the church. There were 1,100 of us in all. The children were with the women. They kept us locked up all morning.

At ten o'clock the soldiers began to kill the men who were in the church. First they machine-gunned them and then they slit their throats.

By two o'clock the soldiers had finished killing the men and they came for the women. They left the children locked up. They separated me from my eight-month-old daughter and my oldest son. They took us away to kill us.

"My God!" I prayed, "Almighty God, do not let us die here! You know that we have committed no sin."

As we came to the place where they were going to kill us, I was able to slip away and hide under a small bush, covering myself with the branches. I watched the soldiers line up twenty women and machine-gun them. Then they brought another group. Another rain of bullets. Then another group. And another.

The women screamed and pleaded: "Don't kill us!"

"We haven't done anything!"

"Why are you going to kill us?"

The soldiers replied, "Stop crying! Don't scream, or the devil will come and take you away!" They continued to kill. I was right there at their feet, hiding.

When the soldiers finished killing the people, they sat down and talked. I heard them say that they had been sent to kill us because we were guerrillas. I watched as they burned all the bodies. When a baby cried out from the midst of the flames, one of the soldiers said to another, "You didn't finish killing him." So the other soldier shot the baby and the crying stopped. When the flames died down, another soldier said,

"They're all dead now. Let's go and kill the children."

They killed four of my children: my nine-year-old, my six-year-old, my three-year-old and my eight-month-old daughter. My husband was killed, too. Only my parents and two of my daughters who lived further away are alive.

I spent seven days and nights alone in the hills with nothing to eat or drink. I couldn't find anyone else; the soldiers had killed everyone.

It has to be God's will that I am still alive. God allowed me to live so that I can testify how the Army killed the men and women and burned their bodies. I didn't see them kill the children, but I heard the children's screams. *April 1987*

SEE HOW THEY SAY TO ME, "WHERE IS THE WORD OF THE LORD? LET IT COME TO PASS!" LET MY PERSECUTORS BE CONFOUNDED, NOT ME; LET THEM, NOT ME, BE TERRIFIED. ON THEM BRING THE DAY OF DISASTER, DESTROY THEM, DESTROY THEM TWICE OVER!

JEREMIAH 17:15,18

d allowed
to live so
at I can
stify how
Army
ed the
n and
men and
ned their
dies.

WHEN WILL OUR SUFFERING END?

The Guazapa volcano, twenty miles north of San Salvador, has been the site of constant Army bombings and ground attacks since 1980. In February 1983, 200 people were massacred in Guadalupe and Tenango, villages on the slopes of the volcano. Each attack raises the civilian death toll and brings another wave of displaced persons to the Church-sponsored shelters in San Salvador.

Julia is a widow who came to the displaced persons camp with her two-year-old granddaughter. Both were severely malnourished. Julia still trembled when she took a spoon in her hand to eat. This is her testimony:

I am grateful that you want to listen to my story. I came to San Salvador a week ago. There have been invasions in Guazapa every two weeks. One day, when the Army began to fire mortars, we fled and hid in an underground shelter. Suddenly there was a lot of shooting and we heard soldiers approaching. They seemed to be everywhere.

"Find the subversives and kill them!" one soldier shouted.

We had to stuff rags in the babies' mouths so they would not make any noise or cry. My little granddaughter passed out for forty minutes. She nearly died of suffocation. Thank God the soldiers left! You cannot imagine how we suffer when we have to cover the children's mouths. But if the soldiers hear any noise, they kill everyone.

Luisa is a young campesina, a woman from the countryside. She lived in a poor village on the lower slopes of the Guazapa volcano where people had little food and no medicine. She came to the displaced persons camp with her five children, her sister and her sister's six children.

We came here fifteen days ago because we could no longer endure the constant invasions and bombings. It is impossible to live in our village anymore. The Army cut down our cornfields and dropped bombs on us. We had nothing to eat. That's why we decided to come here. When we came we carried the two babies while the rest of the children walked.

There was one invasion after another. Once a number of helicopters and planes dropped bombs right on our village. What had we done to deserve such suffering? There used to be 300 families in our village; now there are only ten. Many people died in the invasions or the bombings. My brother-in-law, my sister, three of my sister's children and her mother-in-law were in the house when a bomb blew them to pieces!

In addition to the bombing, the Army often invades and we have to flee. Sometimes we go for as long as twelve days without eating. During the winter, we are exposed to the rain. How the children suffer! But staying at home means death. Even when the Army finds only young children, they cut them to pieces. The Army claims not to harm anyone, but this is a lie. They have killed many people in my village, including elderly people and children.

They say that we are subversives, but that, too, is a lie. My husband was killed by a bomb in the cornfield and now I am alone with all these children. They say that we help the subversives when they come to our villages. That's why the Army cuts down our cornfields. But if we don't have enough food for ourselves to eat, how are we going to help others?

We cannot endure any more suffering. I pray to God that a change will come, and end this injustice. How happy we would be if our liberation would come!   *July 1985*

AND THAT IS WHY I WEEP; MY EYES STREAM WITH WATER, SINCE A COMFORTER WHO COULD REVIVE ME IS FAR AWAY. MY CHILDREN ARE SHATTERED. THE ENEMY HAS PROVED TOO STRONG.

LAMENTATIONS 1:16

You cannot imagine how we suffer when we have to cover the children's mouths. But if the soldiers hear any noise, they kill everyone.

| THE TESTIMONY OF A SURVIVOR

THE LAW OF GOD, THE LAW OF MEN

In El Salvador the army and death squads defend the interests of the wealthy against the poor majority of the country. Every year the Army forcibly recruits 12,000 to 15,000 young men from poor communities to wage the war. The principal targets of the military's strategy are civilians who are accused of providing food, information and logistical support for the guerrillas.

This testimony was given by Laura, a mother of three.

In 1982, when I was pregnant, we were warned that the Army was going to invade our village. We fled to the hills and I gave birth during the flight. Altogether there were six of us: my oldest child, Consuelo, my four-year-old son, Israel, my newborn, my neighbor, Miriam, and her ten-month-old baby. We found a small cave and passed the next eight days in hiding. The children cried a lot. We gave them sugar water to make them sleep.

One morning when we thought the soldiers had gone, Miriam left for the village to bring back diapers, sugar and medicine for the babies. While she was gone, we heard noises outside. Then a soldier pulled back the brush that covered the mouth of the cave and pointed his gun at me.

"No, *señor*, don't kill me," I pleaded.

"What are you doing here, you whore!" he shouted.

"Please, *señor*, don't kill me."

"Then come out of there quickly!" he said.

We left the cave. I saw Miriam. She had been beaten and her hands were tied. There were many armed men—both soldiers and men who I knew were part of the death squad in our village. One of the death squad men ordered Miriam to show them where we had hidden the guns. She told them there were no guns in the cave.

The commander of the soldiers started to interrogate me but he was interrupted by one of the death squad men who whispered something in his ear. The commander pointed to me and ordered the soldiers, "Kill her!" But one soldier objected, "No, not her!"

Another soldier spoke up, "No!"

"No!" said a third soldier.

The soldiers fired shots, but in the air, not at me.

The man from the death squad was furious. He walked over to Miriam, pointed his gun at her and pulled the trigger. When she fell to the ground, he shot her two more times.

The children, thank God, did not even cry. They just stood there in shock. God gave us strength at that moment.

The commander ordered the others to search the cave and remove anything that was there. They threw our clothes and bags near where Miriam lay dead. They gathered everything, even the sugar and diapers which Miriam had brought, and set fire to it all.

These soldiers must have heard Monsignor Romero's voice on the radio when he said, "No soldier is obliged to obey an order against God's law... I beg you, I implore you, I order you, in the name of God, stop the repression!"

They took us to the Army barracks in town. On the way, one of the death squad men said, "We should kill her here. Use this machete."

But a soldier said, "No, we'll take her alive." It could be that when they killed Miriam, their anger was satisfied.

We were held in the Army barracks for nine days. Finally, someone told the Red Cross that we had been captured and the Red Cross came to look for us. We were released and returned home.

I didn't know what to do. It was very dangerous for us in our village. I had my children and Miriam's child, but no clothes and no money. I would have lost my mind if a neighbor had not helped me. She told me, "I am not trying to make you leave—you know I care for you—but hurry! You have to go back to the hills." So I fled once again.

I have always said that soldiers are poor country people like us. Why would they want to kill us? These soldiers must have heard Monsignor Romero's voice on the radio when he said, "No soldier is obliged to obey an order against God's law... I beg you, I implore you, I order you, in the name of God, stop the repression!"
January 1984

SHOULD WE NOURISH ANGER AGAINST OUR FELLOWS AND EXPECT HEALING FROM THE LORD? SHOULD WE REFUSE MERCY TO OUR BROTHERS AND SISTERS YET SEEK PARDON FOR OUR OWN SINS?

SIRACH 28:3-4

A REFLECTION AT THE SITE OF A MASSACRE

THE NEW CALVARY

In September 1988 ten campesinos *were killed by the Salvadoran Army in the village of San Sebastián in the Department of San Vicente. No one has been convicted of the crime. A few days after the massacre, a young man named Carlos returned to the site where the bodies had been found and gave this testimony. Among the victims was his mother.*

When we went to see what had happened, we found that all of the people the Army had captured were dead. Some had been shot in the head, some in other parts of the body. All of their bodies had been mutilated.

They were taken away and killed while still tied up and blindfolded. Look at this blindfold! It is torn up by bullets!

Look at this rock, shattered to pieces by shrapnel! How do you think the people must have looked?

How can anyone believe that these soldiers are doing anything for our country? How can all this killing help our people?

We were afraid and when we came to find their bodies, I was overcome with grief. My mother was found right here. Her sweater was blown off and ended up over there. She must have suffered terribly.

All ten bodies lay right here. These are the leaflets that the guerrillas supposedly left, but we know that they were put there by the soldiers so that they could blame the guerrillas. How could it have been the guerrillas? They don't do this kind of thing. The soldiers left these leaflets behind and said the guerrillas murdered these people. That's a lie.

Look over here at these bouquets of flowers. They were brought by people who came to pray.   *October 1988*

ONCE AGAIN JESUS CRIED OUT IN A LOUD VOICE, AND THEN GAVE UP HIS SPIRIT. MANY BODIES OF SAINTS WHO HAD FALLEN ASLEEP WERE RAISED. AFTER JESUS' RESURRECTION, THEY CAME FORTH FROM THEIR TOMBS AND APPEARED TO MANY.
MATTHEW 27:50,53

A REFLECTION FROM THE PASTORAL CENTER

THE LAW OF SIN IN EL SALVADOR

The Oscar Romero Pastoral Center is a Biblical reflection and training institute of the University of Central America in San Salvador. In this selection written in 1982, the staff of the Pastoral Center offers a reflection on the situation in El Salvador.

In the Bible St. Paul says that death entered the world with sin, and that the wages of sin is death. In El Salvador the law of sin has ruled for many years.

What is the nature of sin in El Salvador? The Legal Aid Office of the Archdiocese of San Salvador reports on human rights abuses and killings by the death squads. Their statistics are conservative because many cases are never reported to any human rights group. In 1981 at least 13,353 people were killed, most of them young men, but also children, women and older people. Usually the killings were preceded by torture or rape. The majority of these crimes were committed by members of the security forces or by paramilitary groups linked to the government.

Recently a great deal of world attention and protest has been focused on human rights violations in Eastern European countries. Many declarations, speeches and threats have been made. But comparatively few people have been killed or imprisoned in these countries. Shouldn't there be a similar response to the oppression in El Salvador where 1 percent of the population has been killed, 20 percent has been displaced or has taken refuge in other countries, and where many political, labor and religious leaders have been imprisoned or killed? *July 1982*

THE WAGES OF SIN IS DEATH, BUT THE GIFT OF GOD IS ETERNAL LIFE IN CHRIST JESUS OUR LORD.

ROMANS 6:23

In El Salvador, 1 percent of the population has been killed; 20 percent has been

Death entered the world with sin, and the wages of sin is death.

displaced or has taken refuge in other countries.

THE TESTIMONY OF A STREET SELLER

DOÑA FRANCISCA'S STORY

The recent history of El Salvador is one of war, torture and killings. We should never forget, though, that the slow death of poverty is as cruel as war for the majority of Salvadorans. Four hundred children die every week of malnutrition.

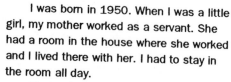

In the market at Santa Tecla, a small city six miles west of San Salvador, Doña Francisca sells yucca roots toasted on her earthen griddle. Four of her grandchildren, all malnourished, run around her, fighting over an old mango seed.

I was born in 1950. When I was a little girl, my mother worked as a servant. She had a room in the house where she worked and I lived there with her. I had to stay in the room all day.

My first child, Elvin, was born when I was 15. I made a little money selling food in a jail. That's where I met the father of my last three children—María, Yanira and Rigoberto. I've suffered a lot trying to raise them. María is sick and lives with me. Yanira goes out with me to sell in order to feed her children. Elvin can't find work, but he makes little things to sell. He doesn't like just sitting around doing nothing.

Life is difficult these days. Money hardly buys anything. If I don't sell anything, I end up in debt. I owe 150 *colones* [about $30] now. How am I ever going to repay that amount? How will I ever get out of debt? I sell mangoes and toasted yucca outside the schools, but I haven't sold anything today or yesterday. I'm desperate. I sell so that we can eat. No sales, no food. There is no other way to survive. So we keep trying to sell toasted yucca; that's our whole life.

When there is no food, like now, we don't know what to do. Sometimes we help the cooks at the market, running errands for them. When that doesn't work, we wash clothes at the river. Somehow we keep going. Often I feel like crying because I know that my grandchildren Carlitos, Chon, María and Paquita are hungry. Poor things. Every morning they ask for bread, but we don't always have any. I ask God to give us food to eat.

I never went to school. With a lot of sacrifice my children completed third grade. It's hard for a mother to see her children suffer. I wonder what my grandchildren would be like if they could go to school. What would it be like if one of them was educated or somehow prepared to make his way in this life? *May 1988*

THEY SHALL NOT HUNGER OR THIRST, NOR SHALL THE SCORCHING WIND OR THE SUN STRIKE THEM. FOR WHOEVER PITIES THEM LEADS THEM AND GUIDES THEM BESIDE SPRINGS OF WATER.

ISAIAH 49:10

I sell so that we can eat. No sales, no food. There is no other way to survive.

So we keep trying to sell toasted yucca; that's our whole life.

TESTIMONIES OF A LAND TAKEOVER

A ROOF OVER OUR HEADS

The city of San Salvador is swollen with more than one hundred thousand people displaced from the countryside by the war. They came seeking the city's relative safety and a new life, but three-quarters of the Salvadoran people cannot find steady work. Most of the displaced live in shantytowns with only a few square feet of ground on which to build a shack.

In one poor community of San Salvador eighty families, compelled by their extreme poverty, decided to take over land owned by the city. Two members of the squatters' community described the situation they fled.

We came here because of the rains. We used to live on the side of a ravine. A few weeks ago it rained three times in a single night and the ground soaked up the water. A mudslide crushed the walls of two houses, burying the families inside. Thank God the neighbors were there and pulled out the families, so no one died. That's why we're here. We came to save ourselves from this danger.

We used to be afraid when the rains came. But we are no longer afraid. We feel more secure now because at least we are on firm ground. On the hillside we lived in danger of landslides. Now when we go to sleep, we don't worry, even if it rains a lot.

Before coming here, we used to get up in the night whenever it rained, because we thought the walls would collapse in the strong winds and rain. Now we feel safer.

However, we have no security here. We don't own this land. It belongs to the city, and the mayor has not responded positively to our requests to stay. Will we be able to stay here or will the government level our houses?   *July 1987*

THEY PASSED THE NIGHT NAKED, WITHOUT CLOTHING, FOR THEY HAVE NO COVERING AGAINST THE COLD; THEY ARE DRENCHED WITH THE RAIN OF THE MOUNTAINS, AND FOR WANT OF SHELTER THEY CLING TO THE ROCK.

JOB 24:7-8

THE TESTIMONY OF A TEN-YEAR-OLD

DELMI AND HER BROTHERS

Delmi is a ten-year-old girl from the countryside. Like thousands of other Salvadoran children, she has suffered the horrors of war. She and her two brothers, three-year-old Saúl and six-year-old Mauricio, are orphans. They fled the countryside after soldiers killed their mother.

They eventually found refuge in one of the camps for displaced people opened by Archbishop Romero. Delmi is now responsible for her two little brothers. She is their "papá" and "mamá."

One day my *mamá* went down to the river to wash. She took my brother Saúl with her. My *papá* was in the house lying down because he had twisted his ankle in the hills. As I lit the fire to cook, I looked up and saw armed men approaching our house. My brother Mauricio ran to *papá* and told him, "The soldiers are coming!"

Papá didn't want anything to happen to us. He was about to run, but I told him, "Hide! I'll tell them you are not here."

When the soldiers came to the house, they asked me, "Where is your *papá*?"

I told them, "He left days ago to look for work."

"Don't lie!" they said. "If you won't tell us where he is, you're going to be sorry!"

I looked at the soldiers and then at Mauricio. I was afraid he would tell them where *papá* was. Mauricio kept glancing in the direction where *papá* was hiding. The soldiers entered the house and pushed me to the floor. They looked around, but they did not find *papá*. Mauricio clung to my dress. We were terrified.

The men went outside, furious, and asked for *mamá*. I said that she had gone to town. They told me to give them some water. I wanted them to go away, but I gave them something to drink. Then they left.

Papá was safe. But later our neighbors came to the house and said that *mamá* was dead in the ravine. Some of the neighbors had seen the soldiers drag my *mamá* away and do terrible things to her. Then they killed her.

Later, the neighbors buried *mamá*. *Papá* gathered our clothes and blankets and the photograph of their wedding and brought us to our godmother's house. Then he went to the mountains. A little while ago we heard that he had been killed, but we don't know if that is true. Maybe he will come to look for us or maybe he's dead.
April 1982

WOE TO THOSE WHO ENACT UNJUST STATUTES AND WHO WRITE OPPRESSIVE DECREES... MAKING WIDOWS THEIR PLUNDER, AND ORPHANS THEIR PREY!
ISAIAH 10:1A,2B

A Story of Sugarcane Workers

ONLY OUR LIVES TO OFFER

Historically, El Salvador has suffered from the greatest inequality of land ownership in Latin America. This situation deteriorated through the 1970s to the point that six families of the oligarchy owned more land than 133,000 farming families. Forty percent of all campesinos had no land at all. Large plantations dominate the fertile lands, producing cotton, coffee, and sugarcane for export, while the poor are landless and their children go hungry.

Since their youth, Graciela and Ramón had worked in the sugarcane fields. Wages were very low and they had a difficult time feeding their eight children.

On numerous occasions they protested their starvation wages, but with no success. In 1979, driven by desperation, Ramón participated in a land takeover. The plantation owners called in the National Guard to resolve the conflict quickly. More than 200 workers were machine-gunned to death, Ramón among them.

After the massacre, Graciela and her family, along with many of their neighbors, fled to the hills. The National Guard pursued them, killing entire families.

Ramón and Graciela's three oldest children—two boys and a girl—joined the FMLN guerrillas. Graciela and her five younger children found sanctuary in a displaced persons camp in San Salvador.

The war destroyed entire villages in the countryside, but the FMLN was soon strong enough to hold back large-scale Army invasions in some areas. A group of displaced people from Graciela's village decided to return home. Graciela and her children joined them.

Although the government forces could not advance on the ground, they could attack from the air. The Air Force bombed the repopulated zones to prevent people from returning. A few weeks after she had returned home, they attacked Graciela's village. Women, elderly people and children died. Graciela's baby was killed by mortar shrapnel as the family was fleeing the attack. "I heard a great explosion," she said. "When I looked at my baby, I saw that he had been cut in half, right in my arms."

Graciela felt that she could not survive her baby's death. "I suffered so much that I did not want to live anymore. I didn't know what to do. I went for days without eating or sleeping. I prayed to the Virgin Mary for nine days. She consoled me and gave me the strength to live."

Graciela and her four youngest children fled once again to the displaced persons camp where she awaits news of her three children who are fighting. She prays the rosary to the Virgin every night to keep her hope alive. After all that has happened to her, she said, "I feel now that I am ready to give up my life, and even the lives of my children, for the liberation of our people."
August 1981

MOST ADMIRABLE AND WORTHY OF EVER-LASTING REMEMBRANCE WAS THE MOTHER, WHO SAW HER SEVEN SONS PERISH IN A SINGLE DAY, YET BORE IT COURAGEOUSLY BECAUSE OF HER HOPE IN THE LORD.
II MACCABEES 7:20

The Testimony of a Catechist

A CALL TO SERVE

The only contact many people in the countryside have with a priest is during the yearly feast day of their village's patron saint. After the Medellín Conference of Latin American Bishops in 1968, the role of laypeople in the Church changed. Lay ministers, known as catechists or delegates of the Word, accepted responsibility for pastoral work in many communities. The Church became a church of the poor in these communities, its theology grounded in everyday experience.

In this narrative, a catechist, Magdalena, shared her testimony.

My husband was a catechist. He tried to serve everyone and the whole community trusted him. On Sunday our house was a meeting place for young people who came to hear my husband talk about the Word of God.

After a while some people began to say that those of us who had Bibles or sang songs about Monsignor Romero or had pictures of him were subversives.

When I took lunch to my husband in the fields, he would talk to me about what I should do if he were killed. He said, "If I'm killed, don't cry for me. Rejoice if something happens to me or they kill me. You are brave. Be an example to the others. I don't live just for the sake of being alive. Christ gave me life and he may take it from me. I am ready to give up my life."

One day, my husband was working in the fields with two other men and a child. The military came and took their identity documents. Other soldiers then came and said that people without identity papers were subversives. The soldiers dragged my husband and the three others to a ravine. They cut their throats. Our neighbors overcame their fear and asked the local military commander for permission to bury the bodies. All of them, including the child, were buried in a common grave.

After this, no one in our village wanted to talk to anyone else. The soldiers said that if anything was said about the deaths, they would cut the throats of the people who had spoken. No one said anything. Everyone was afraid. Even my next-door neighbor, who was the mother of the two men who were killed with my husband, would not talk to us about the killings. She did not want to be seen speaking to us because she had other children and she was afraid that if she spoke on behalf of the ones who had been killed, the others might be killed as well. Some people defended my husband and the other men saying, "They were on the side of the poor." Other people said, "They were subversives and communists." Everyone was afraid. A few days afterwards, we left the area, but later we returned. What could we do so far away?

After this, people continued to come to my house. I realized that it was up to me to continue my husband's work. His courage gave me strength.

> We used to think that being a catechist just meant talking about the Word of God. At that time the people just listened. But my husband and others taught us that we must work for the community and help those who need us.

There was a great need for catechists to work with the community because the priest only comes here once in a while. A group of us thought about how we could continue working as we had done when my husband was alive. Not just by going to other communities to talk about the Word of God, but by helping people. We used to think that being a catechist just meant talking about the Word of God. At that time the people just listened. But my husband and others taught us that we must work for the community and help those who need us. So today we visit the communities, we learn about their problems, and we help them.

The FMLN asked me to work with them because they said that I could help. But I told them that I felt a different calling. I prefer to work the way that my husband taught me, as a catechist, teaching the Word of God. Not just speaking the Word, but living it by working for the poor and urging my brothers and sisters to commit themselves to this work as well.

There is one thing that the Gospel commands which I have not done: leave my children and my parents for the Gospel. But God, our Lord, has to understand that I have to raise the children because my husband is not with us and I have to work to support them. But Saturdays and Sundays I take the Word of God to neighboring communities. *April 1984*

AND SOME SEED FELL INTO GOOD SOIL AND GREW AND PRODUCED ITS CROP A HUNDREDFOLD.

LUKE 8:8

WITH GOD AND A MEDICAL KIT IN THE MOUNTAINS

Following the brutal repression of popular protest in the early 1980s, thousands of campesinos, *union members, students and teachers were forced to leave the country, go underground, or take up arms in a revolutionary struggle against the government. These men and women, who share a commitment to political struggle, refer to each other as "compañeros."*

In this testimony, Teresa, who joined the guerillas in 1981 to work as a nurse in a war zone, tells her story.

When I was still living in San Salvador, I was once detained by two men from the security forces. They forced me at gunpoint to go with them to a vacant lot. They threatened to kill me. I could not escape. I cried and prayed, but they just taunted me. They threw me down on the ground and raped me until I fainted. After I regained consciousness, I was sick for eight days.

Later, when I told my *compañeros* what had happened, they told me that the hatred I felt for my assailants would give me strength for my work. But I disagreed. I will always remember their faces, but I cannot hate them.

After that, I decided to come here to the mountains to work as a nurse. At first when there was combat, I was very frightened. I prayed to God, asking for courage. Then I felt more confident that God would help me to continue my work here, taking care of the sick and wounded.

I remember that once in the midst of a bombing, a woman began to give birth. The air raid warning had been given and everyone was running to the bomb shelter because the planes were coming. I tried to help the woman reach the bomb shelter, but she couldn't make it. We moved under a tree. The baby was born there as the bombs exploded around us. I was half-dead with fear. My legs wanted to run to the bomb shelter, but how could I leave the woman? The attack lasted an hour. We couldn't even cover the baby. There was dust in the air from the bombs, and the baby was in danger of getting tetanus. But, thanks to God, the mother and baby survived.

I also remember an evacuation. There were more than 200 people, including children, pregnant women, elderly people and sick people. We hid during the day because planes were flying over us. At night we walked and walked. We had nothing to eat except a small spoonful of honey two or three times a day. We drank from streams. We couldn't light a fire because the smoke would have given away our location to the planes. At night, we suffered terribly from the cold. I thought about the people who followed Jesus and slept outdoors and shared whatever they had. Thinking about this enabled me to keep on going.

Although we are fighting a war, we are not doing so because of hatred. We are motivated not by hatred but by a desire for a better world. God willing, this war will end.
September 1981

YOUR STRENGTH DOES NOT LIE IN NUMBERS, NOR YOUR MIGHT IN STRONG MEN; SINCE YOU ARE THE GOD OF THE HUMBLE, THE HELP OF THE OPPRESSED, THE SUPPORT OF THE WEAK, THE REFUGE OF THE FORSAKEN, THE SAVIOUR OF THE DESPAIRING.

JUDITH 9:11

THE FAITH OF AN FMLN COMBATANT

WHY WE STRUGGLE

Who are the guerrillas in El Salvador? Why are they fighting? What is their vision? In this testimony Daniel, a former university student, shares his Christian faith.

My faith led me to join the armed struggle. I believe that God loves the poor. That is why I felt my Christian duty was to witness to the teachings of Christ. One Gospel text, Matthew 25, has always been particularly important to me. The Lord asks how we can love God—whom we do not see—and not love our brother or sister whom we see every day. I came to the conclusion that faith must be expressed in love for our brothers and sisters, particularly the poor and the oppressed. In El Salvador there is no way to escape this conclusion: the Gospel leads to a total commitment to the revolutionary struggle.

Our goal is to radically transform this society. We shouldn't have to achieve this through armed struggle, but that is the only option left. We want to transform a society which produces only hunger, unemployment and death into a society which promotes life. In El Salvador, for example, many children die from diseases which can be prevented or cured. We want a society in which such unnecessary deaths do not occur.

I don't see any real difference between believers and non-believers who are part of the revolutionary struggle. Our way of life is exactly the same. Both those who consider themselves non-believers and love the people, and those who consider themselves Christians give up their lives with the same generosity as Christ did.

A guerrilla's life is difficult. It demands constant movement and exposure to the elements; one endures the cold, the damp and the rain. It is a life of fear because of the bombings, the strafing and ambushes. We often find ourselves surrounded by thousands of soldiers. Fear is the inseparable companion of a guerrilla. I say this so that you may understand that one does not become a guerrilla because of courage, but because of conscience.   *June 1986*

JUDAS MACCABEUS AND HIS COMPANIONS ENTERED THE VILLAGES SECRETLY AND SUMMONED THEIR KINSMEN. THEY IMPLORED GOD TO LOOK KINDLY UPON THE PEOPLE, WHO WERE BEING OPPRESSED ON ALL SIDES, TO REMEMBER THE CRIMINAL SLAUGHTER OF INNOCENT CHILDREN AND TO MANIFEST GOD'S HATRED OF EVIL.

II MACCABEES 8:1A,2A,4

| THE FAITH OF AN FMLN COMBATANT

WE, TOO, BELIEVE IN GOD

Since the 1960s, profound changes have taken place in the Church in Latin America. In the Conferences of Latin American Bishops held at Medellín and Puebla, the Bishops concluded that Christians should work with the poor for the cause of justice. In this testimony, Beto relates the story of the transformation of his life and faith.

I have been in the struggle for nine years. I left my work, my home, and my children in order to dedicate myself to our people's liberation.

In the late 1960s and the early 1970s I was a catechist. Often I went to the church to teach catechism after I had been drinking. I also did other things that were wrong.

I told the children that God punishes and that God must be respected, but I never told them that to love God, we must also love our neighbor. I taught the children the same doctrines that I had been taught. I never told them that we live in a corrupt society ruled by hatred and selfishness.

Later I saw others—laypeople, priests and nuns—teach a more profound and humane religion based on our experience. Our martyrs—Monsignor Romero, Fathers Rutilio Grande, Octavio Ortiz and Rafael Palacios—set an example for us. I under-stood how I had been indoctrinated by my grandmother and the people who taught me catechism and how I had taught the same things to the children. I really felt ashamed.

As I came to know the poor I also came to know Christ. I now see Christ in a new way. I see him in the *campesino* working with his hoe and in the boy selling newspapers on the streets of San Salva-dor. I see him wherever our people suffer, sweating at my side in factories and suffering abuse and injustice.

In the FMLN we all struggle together. We take every opportunity to talk to the people, many of whom think in the old ways. When they ask if we believe in God, I tell them, "Yes, we believe in God, and we see Christ in the people." This has helped to counteract the lies of our enemies which are intended to keep the poorest people ignorant so that they will not support our struggle. The people themselves are beginning to realize that what our enemies say is not true.

We believe in a living God. We follow the example of our martyrs, especially our beloved pastor, Monsignor Romero.
September 1986

BECAUSE HE DISPENSED JUSTICE TO THE WEAK AND THE POOR, IT WENT WELL WITH HIM. IS THIS NOT TRUE KNOWLEDGE OF ME? SAYS THE LORD.

JEREMIAH 22:16

DIARY EXCERPT OF A PRIEST IN A WAR ZONE

BETO'S WATCH

In the Department of Chalatenango, two authorities exercise military and political control: the government and the FMLN. Although the people live at a subsistence level, they say that life is better under FMLN control. The FMLN forces landowners to pay a just wage to the workers. The people have more freedom to organize themselves for health care, for education, and in cooperatives.

The following story is about Beto whose testimony appears in the previous selection. In this account a parish priest in Chalatenango describes Beto's death.

Somewhere in El Salvador, a soldier has a watch that I bought years ago in a foreign country. I don't know who this soldier is, but I know that I didn't buy the watch for him. I bought it for Beto, one of the many friends I have made in my ministry here in Chalatenango. This is the story of how a soldier came to have Beto's watch.

Like most guerrillas, Beto was a farmworker. When I met him, he was in charge of the political work in the area where we lived. He knew everyone, and visited people in their homes. Everyone trusted him. He was always fair, and people said he was humble. He loved to play soccer, and I remember one day after a game he told me, "I'm getting too old for

this, Father." He was about 38 years old at the time.

Once in a while I would see Chana, his wife. Chana lived in another village. She always told me to tell Beto how much she loved him. When I would see Beto, I would tell him, "Hugs and kisses from the other side of the mountain." "Thank you, Father," he would answer with a shy smile. When I saw Chana again I would tell her the same thing, "Hugs and kisses from the far side of the mountain."

A few days ago I met Chana on the road. We greeted one another and walked together for a long time in silence. Suddenly she said, "You didn't send me hugs and kisses, Father."

I did not know what to tell her. We kept our sadness inside as we walked together. Beto had been killed two months before in front of the store where we gathered to listen to the World Cup soccer games. He was leaving the store when soldiers appeared and began to shoot. Beto and a twelve-year-old girl were shot in the back. The girl died immediately, but Beto fell to the ground, wounded.

"My God, my God!" he murmured from the ground. One of the soldiers said to him mockingly, "You'd do better to call for a nurse." Then he pointed his rifle at Beto's face and blew it to pieces. As a prize, they

gave Beto's watch to the soldier who had
shot him in the face. Then they divided up
the rest of the spoils. When they left, Beto
was buried with just his pants and shirt.

I often recall Beto's shy smile when I
brought him "hugs and kisses" from Chana,
and I wonder who has his watch. *May 1988*

WHEN THEY HAD CRUCIFIED HIM, THEY
DIVIDED HIS CLOTHES AMONG THEM BY
CASTING LOTS.

MATTHEW 27:35

DIARY EXCERPT OF A PRIEST IN A WAR ZONE

DEATH BEFORE THEIR TIME

The same parish priest whose diary was excerpted in the previous selection offers this account of his pastoral ministry in the Department of Chalatenango.

The Salvadoran people have a Biblical sense of time. "There is a time for everything under the sun." Today it seems to be a time to die. So many deaths, among them Rosita and María.

Early yesterday morning, I took a walk along a rugged stretch of country road with a young friend. It was a beautiful morning and I was enjoying the walk. Suddenly we heard shooting and mortar-fire on the other side of the hill. My friend and I found shelter and waited until the fighting had ended.

During the day I heard that five people had been killed and their bodies left at the exact spot where three young guerrillas had been killed last year. Those three young men's bodies had been eaten by pigs, and I was concerned that this would happen again. After Mass I tried to find out what had happened. I was unable to learn anything further, however, so I returned to see for myself. The rumors were true. Close to where I had turned back, I found the bullet-riddled bodies of five young guerrillas lying on the road. I recognized two of them, Rosita and María.

Rosita's mother is a well-known leader of the revolutionary organization in this area. She is a practicing Christian and has been a catechist. Rosita's father and I had a long talk a little while ago. He told me that he used to think that everything was God's will, but after he studied the Bible with others, his eyes were opened. I only met Rosita recently. She was dressed like a guerrilla. She came up to me and introduced herself shyly, "I am Rosita, the daughter of Sara and Marcos." She had the same welcoming smile as her mother. The last time I saw her was a few weeks ago when she read the first reading at Mass.

María was 30 years old. Before joining the guerrillas she was a teacher. Later she had both political and military responsibilities with the FMLN. We came to know one another a few months ago when a problem arose in one of the villages. I protested an incident in which I felt the guerrillas had acted unjustly. María listened to me and then publicly apologized to the people. I saw María for the last time two weeks ago when she asked if she could use my shower. We said good-bye with the customary "Go with God!" and "Take care!"

Rosita and María's boots and personal possessions had been taken from their bodies, and María's dress was ripped. I covered her and went to the next village to look for men to bury the bodies. Although they were afraid, several men did come out to dig a grave. We put María, Rosita and their three companions in this common grave. It rained as we prayed for them—the first rain of the season.   *September 1987*

A SAMARITAN WHO WAS JOURNEYING ALONG CAME ON HIM AND WAS MOVED TO PITY AT THE SIGHT.

LUKE 10:33

A DEVOTION BY THE MOTHERS OF THE DISAPPEARED

MARY, OUR MODEL OF ACCOMPANIMENT

In El Salvador, government security forces and death squads have been responsible for the disappearance of more than seven thousand people. Their bodies have never been found. Encouraged by Archbishop Romero, their mothers and family members organized the "Committee of the Mothers and Relatives of the Disappeared, Political Prisoners and Assassinated of El Salvador - Monsignor Oscar Arnulfo Romero." This organization, known as COMADRES, struggles for an end to human rights violations.

In this selection, COMADRES members offer a devotion during Mass.

Today we commemorate Our Lady of Mount Carmel who accompanied her son from birth to death and was present at his resurrection. She did not ask what she was going to suffer along the way, nor did she stop to think of the dangers. She simply accompanied him through life to the glory of his resurrection.

Today, she is our model. As families of political prisoners and the disappeared, we want to publicly renew our promise to accompany our loved ones in the struggle for liberation. We call on all people of good will to share our hope and join our struggle: a hope born of God, a struggle which unites the People of God.

Our strength and commitment come from a profound conviction that we are called to give up our lives for each other. We are called to defend the dignity of all men and women against tyranny, exploitation and oppression.

God, in whose image and likeness we are made, nurtures this conviction. God teaches us the great commandment of love. Jesus offers us the example of what it means to give up one's life for others. Christ's resurrection from the dead gives us hope for the coming of the kingdom of solidarity, justice and peace.

For this reason, we gather around the altar to celebrate the Eucharist together, in memory of his passion, death and resurrection, the root of our strength and the source of our hope.   *August 1982*

NEAR THE CROSS OF JESUS THERE STOOD HIS MOTHER, HIS MOTHER'S SISTER, MARY THE WIFE OF CLOPAS AND MARY MAGDALENE.

JOHN 19:25

A EULOGY BY HIS WIDOW

HERBERT ANAYA: *PRESENTE!*

Herbert Anaya, president of the non-governmental Human Rights Commission of El Salvador (CDHES), was assassinated by a death squad on October 26, 1987. He was the seventh member of the Commission to have been killed since its founding in 1978. Surrounded by her five children, Anaya's widow, Mirna, spoke from the altar at his funeral in the Cathedral in San Salvador.

People of El Salvador, a thousand times heroic!

At this time, so filled with pain and grief by the separation from my husband, I thank you for being here. You feel as I do, and as so many of our people who cannot be with us today feel. You gave my husband the opportunity to voice your suffering and your anguish. Without you, he would not have been what he was. He was humble, and you inspired him to give his life for all of us. You gave him courage by your example.

I also thank everyone who has come from outside the country to share in our suffering. I thank you for your demonstration of solidarity with my family and the Human Rights Commission. I want to remind you that our people continue to suffer. They need your support. You must continue to lift up your voices to denounce the oppression.

I repeat the call of Archbishop Romero. I plead with those of you who are members of the security forces. Stop killing your brothers and sisters. We are poor, just like you. Stop this killing!

I do not ask for vengeance against those who assassinated my husband. Herbert never hated them. If he could speak today, he would forgive them. But he would also demand, with the same courage that he always demonstrated, that they stop killing their brothers and sisters.
October 1987

THINK OF THE WAY HE PERSEVERED AGAINST SUCH OPPOSITION FROM SINNERS AND THEN YOU WILL NOT LOSE HEART AND COME TO GRIEF. IN THE FIGHT AGAINST SIN, YOU HAVE NOT YET HAD TO KEEP FIGHTING TO THE POINT OF BLOODSHED.
HEBREWS 12:1A,3-4

REMEMBERING ARCHBISHOP OSCAR ROMERO

During his years as Archbishop of San Salvador, Monsignor Oscar Romero lived in a cottage adjacent to a cancer hospital staffed by Carmelite nuns. One of the sisters, a close friend of Monsignor Romero, was present at the Mass in the hospital chapel when Romero was assassinated on March 24, 1980. She offered this testimony about his life.

Monsignor Romero's last homily was beautiful. He spoke as if he knew that he was going to be killed. He said several times that if a grain of wheat does not die, it cannot bear fruit. When he finished his homily, he walked to the center of the sanctuary. A second later, we heard a shot.

I thank God for that great prophet of El Salvador. He died as Christ died. Today he intercedes for all the poor and for all his flock.

A journalist once asked Monsignor Romero if he was afraid when he denounced injustice and abuses. Monsignor said that he was afraid and that he

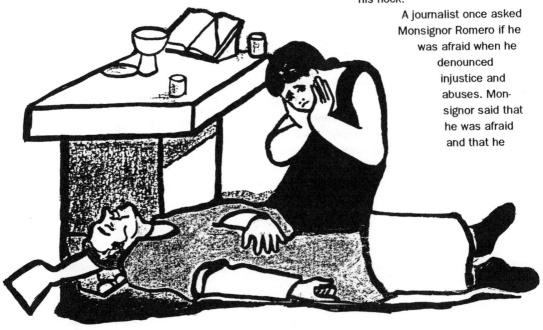

knew what was going to happen to him. He also said that he forgave those who were going to kill him. He knew that he would be resurrected in his people.

We should all have this faith and hope and love.

We have already witnessed Monsignor's resurrection in the people's faith and in their hope that one day things will change.

The grains of wheat are bearing fruit. Monsignor suffered from seeing so much injustice, so much death, so much of his people's blood shed. He often felt powerless. But now that he is near to God, he is able to do much.

We must be patient, and have faith in God and the Virgin Mary, the Queen of Peace, to whom Monsignor was so devoted. We are sure that one day we will live in peace. Until then, we hope for the day when everyone will love each other.   *April 1985*

I SOLEMNLY ASSURE YOU, UNLESS THE GRAIN OF WHEAT FALLS TO THE EARTH AND DIES, IT REMAINS JUST A GRAIN OF WHEAT. BUT IF IT DIES, IT PRODUCES MUCH FRUIT.

JOHN 12:24

PROFESSION OF FAITH OF THE CHRISTIAN BASE COMMUNITIES

Beginning in 1969, the movement of Christian base communities took root in the poor communities of El Salvador. Small groups gather, often in their homes, to study the Bible and celebrate the sacraments as communities of faith. Their discussions lead to new interpretations of the Gospel based on their daily experiences, and to new understandings of their situation, illuminated by Scripture reflection.

The Christian base communities have been attacked for their devotion to the Gospel. Christ the Saviour church in the Zacamil district of San Salvador was bombed in 1980 and remained closed for four years. In November 1989 the church was desecrated again by Army troops who violated the tabernacle and scattered the Blessed Sacrament on the floor. The following prayer was offered by the people of the parish to commemorate the fifteenth anniversary of the Christian base communities in Zacamil on February 12, 1984. The church was decorated with red flowers in memory of the 623 martyrs from this parish. The Eucharist was celebrated by a thousand people, among them twelve priests and the Archbishop.

WE BELIEVE in God,
who created us free and walks with us in the struggle for liberation.

WE BELIEVE in Christ,
crucified again in the suffering of the poor, a suffering which calls out to the conscience of people and nations, a suffering which ends in resurrection.

WE BELIEVE in the power of the Spirit,
capable of inspiring the same compassion which has led our best brothers and sisters to martyrdom.

WE BELIEVE in the Church,
called forth by Jesus and by the Holy Spirit.

WE BELIEVE that when we gather,
Jesus is with us, Mary, our Mother, is at our side, a sign of faithfulness to the Lord.

WE BELIEVE in the Christian community
where we proclaim our ideals, through which we practice our Christian faith.

WE BELIEVE in building a Church
where we pray and reflect on our reality, and share in the prophetic, priestly and pastoral mission of Jesus.

In this way we make the Kingdom of
God present on earth.

WE BELIEVE in unity in the midst
of differences.

WE BELIEVE that Christ calls us
to communion and to live as sisters and
brothers.

WE BELIEVE that we need
to love one another, to correct one
another compassionately, to forgive
each other's errors and weaknesses.

WE BELIEVE that we need
to help one another recognize our
limitations, to support each other in the
faith.

WE BELIEVE that the poor,
the illiterate and the sick, the perse-
cuted and tortured, are closest to the
Gospel of Jesus. Through them, Christ
challenges us to work for justice and
peace. Their cause is our cause.

WE BELIEVE that Christ is also present
in those who are slaves to their pas-
sions, to vices, lies and injustice, to
power and money.

WE COMMIT ourselves
to never give up hope in the possibility of
their conversion; to love them even
though they slander, persecute and kill
us; to pray for them and to help them so
that one day they may live simply and
humbly in the way that the Gospel calls
all of us to live. Amen

February 1984

FOR IT IS YOUR SPECIAL PRIVILEGE TO TAKE
CHRIST'S PART, NOT ONLY TO BELIEVE IN HIM
BUT ALSO TO SUFFER FOR HIM.

PHILIPPIANS 1:29

A RECOLLECTION OF A CHRISTMAS LITURGY

WHERE CHRIST WAS BORN

A North American priest visited a displaced persons refuge in San Salvador in 1981 and wrote the following reflection.

This year I celebrated Christmas Mass with more than 200 displaced people living in the basement of a church in San Salvador.

These people cannot leave the church. Many have been here for a year and a half. During this time they have not seen the sunlight or taken a breath of fresh air. They have organized themselves into groups to cook, clean, take care of the children, and stand watch. Nine children have been born here and the community is now expecting four more.

Over the table that served as our altar the people hung a large newspaper photograph of Archbishop Romero. Even in death Romero continues to be present to the people. "Monsignor visited our village," they told me. "He was one of us. His memory is our most treasured possession."

Next to the photograph of Archbishop Romero was a faded image of the Sacred Heart of Jesus. Both images served as silent acolytes during our Eucharistic celebration. People offered petitions and thanks and prayed for their dead. They prayed for their children and relatives, and for the nuns who share their lives with them. They also thanked God for many things, especially for life.

It was evident from their prayers that they find encouragement and hope in their belief that Jesus loves them. They believe in Jesus the liberator and saviour.

As I shared the Christmas celebration with these displaced people, it was easy to imagine Jesus being born in a church basement like this one, amidst the smell of *tamales* and the strumming of two old guitars. Here, Jesus would have been at home.   *December 1981*

SHE WRAPPED HIM IN SWADDLING CLOTHES AND LAID HIM IN A MANGER BECAUSE THERE WAS NO ROOM FOR THEM IN THE INN.

LUKE 2:7

A RECOLLECTION OF A PASTORAL VISIT

THE DAY OF THE CROSS IN USULUTAN

Thousands of people displaced by the war are trying to rebuild their lives and communities throughout El Salvador. Something new is being born, a new experience of faith in the midst of war. The following is the testimony of a pastoral worker who visited several communities in the Department of Usulután and joined in their religious celebration.

Salvadorans find hope in the midst of death because life is stronger than death. Despite the fact that their lives are in danger, the people in each of these communities share an irrepressible hope.

On May 3, the Feast of the Holy Cross, the people rose early to cut flowers and build little altars in front of their homes. They decorated the crosses on these altars with flowers.

That afternoon the community had a Celebration of the Word beginning with a procession through the village. Flowers were hung everywhere. A little girl invited me to sing with the people. All the children sang, their voices a beautiful contrast to the distant explosions of mortars and bombs.

Many people from distant villages came to the Celebration of the Word. They were happy because they had not celebrated for a long time. They say that the

Church has abandoned them.

"Priests won't come here because they are afraid of the Army," one woman told me. People do not talk about this with resentment, but with pain. They are Christians and want to celebrate Mass.

The Celebration of the Word focused on the text from Luke's Gospel where Jesus says, "The Spirit of the Lord is upon me, to announce good news to the poor, liberation to the captives, and liberty to the oppressed." These words found an echo in these displaced people—poor, captive, and oppressed. Their commentaries were simple, and to the point, "We have faith because Jesus is on the side of the poor."

Later in the evening a woman came to tell us that a child had died in a nearby community. The people immediately organized to help the bereaved family.

In the midst of war they celebrate their faith in song, in word and by acts of love.
May 1986

GO AND REPORT TO JOHN WHAT YOU HAVE SEEN AND HEARD. THE BLIND RECOVER THEIR SIGHT, CRIPPLES WALK, LEPERS ARE CURED, THE DEAF HEAR, THE DEAD ARE RAISED TO LIFE, AND THE POOR HAVE THE GOOD NEWS PREACHED TO THEM.

LUKE 7:22

THE TESTIMONY OF A PERSECUTED COMMUNITY

SONIA'S BAPTISM

In another story of a guinda, or forced flight, because of an Army invasion, the people paused to rest and to baptize and receive a new member into their community.

It was six o'clock in the morning on February 28, 1983. We found shelter by the side of a creek in a deep ravine. We had been walking since the 25th, fleeing the bombing. On the afternoon of the 25th, a 250-pound bomb killed a woman who was carrying her baby girl. The father pulled his two-month-old daughter from the dead mother's arms and had been carrying the child for the last three days.

We gathered in the shadow of the trees to baptize the infant. José, a seminarian, spoke.

"We are going to participate in one of the most beautiful acts of our Church—baptism. We will give a name to this little girl who three days ago lost her mother.

"Christianity has humble origins. But Christianity has been betrayed because at times the Church has been, and still is, characterized by wealth and pomp. This is because of King Constantine who gave the Church great power so that it would support him. The Church thought that having power and wealth and great cathedrals and schools would build the Kingdom of God. But if we go back to the origin of our faith and to the life of the one who is our friend, the founder of our Church, our companion and our older brother, Jesus Christ, we see that he was poor, like us."

Then Father Tilo added, "As José has said, I invite you to share in this beautiful ceremony. We are going to use the symbol of water. But first let me ask you: Who knows the value of water? What does water mean to you?"

One person answered, "Water is essential to life. We can go for days without eating. But if we don't have water, we will die."

Father Tilo continued, "That's right. The river has given us life for the past three days. Now it is going to be a symbol of the life we are giving to this little girl as we

> It is the community which takes
> care of Sonia and of all children in the world.
> We are making this revolution for them.
> A revolution would not be worth the
> sacrifices if it were not for the children.

receive her into our community. During these past three days, when one person has eaten, everyone has eaten. When one person has had water to drink, everyone has had water to drink. Today we are not only going to baptize this little girl, we are also going to make her a member of our community. She will suffer what we suffer. She will struggle as we struggle and win the same freedom as all of us on the day of our victory. What name are we going to give her?"

Her father answered, "Sonia."

"On behalf of Sonia, on behalf of all the children, on behalf of all the orphans, on behalf of all the baptized, we are going to pray to you, Lord, the prayer of all your children, the Lord's Prayer."

Before pouring the water, Father Tilo reminded us, "Let us remember that in a liberated community all of us are the child's godparents. It is the community which takes care of Sonia and of all children in the world. We are making this revolution for them. A revolution would not be worth the sacrifices if it were not for the children."

And this is how Sonia was baptized, with water from a stream, as her community gathered in a ravine.   *April 1983*

IF THE RAISING OF THE DEAD IS NOT A REALITY, WHY BE BAPTIZED ON THEIR BEHALF? AND WHY ARE WE CONTINUALLY PUTTING OURSELVES IN SUCH DANGER?
I CORINTHIANS 15:29B-30A

The Confession of a Persecuted Community

FOR WE HAVE SINNED

When the Army invades a village, the people flee, often spending days or weeks hiding in the mountains. During one of these forced flights—which are called guindas—the people took time to repent for their sins.

We arrived at a rocky slope covered with brush after walking in ravines and along rough paths for three days. Two members of the pastoral team invited us to give thanks to God for having saved us from the enemy and to recall our sins.

We began by making the sign of the cross. Then Juan, one of the community's catechists, asked us to recall our personal sins. At first there was silence. Then an elderly woman spoke.

"The enemy is killing us."

Juan answered, "Yes, that is terrible. But right now let us think about our own sins, those we committed while fleeing."

There was more silence until a child said, "Fear."

"It's true that we have been afraid," Juan said. "But fear is not a sin. We sin if we give up because of fear, if we lose hope that God is with us."

Gradually all of us became calm. We quietly reflected on our sins. After a short while someone said, "I didn't want to bury the dead."

All of us had felt the same. While we were fleeing, some people who had been killed had been left unburied. One person said, "But the bodies really stank."

The children laughed. But Juan replied, "Children, think about how terrible it is to have so many dead bodies and no one to bury them. There are no cemeteries here. It becomes an act of mercy just to bury our dead."

Someone else said, "Some of us had a little bread and others did not. Many people hid their bread even though they saw other people going hungry."

We continued to recall selfish things that we had done—our sins—and we asked God to forgive us, singing, "Lord, have mercy on your people."   *May 1983*

Then I acknowledged my sin to you, my guilt I covered not. I said, "I confess my faults to the Lord," and you took away the guilt of my sin.

Psalms 32:5

A DEFENSE OF THE CHRISTIAN BASE COMMUNITIES

A NEW EXPRESSION OF CHURCH

In this selection, the staff of the Oscar Romero Pastoral Center reflect on the promise of the church of the poor.

The Church continues to grow in the Christian base communities. Some people say that the base communities are trying to create a parallel church opposed to the hierarchy. Others claim that the base communities are overly involved in politics. The facts are that the base communities have publicly supported the declarations of the hierarchy in favor of a dialogue for peace, and actively engage in dialogue with priests and bishops.

The base communities are committed to their people's struggle for liberation. This commitment inevitably involves them in politics. Church involvement in political activity is legitimate, within certain limits.

Now, more than ever, the Church of El Salvador needs unity. The Christian base communities have the capacity to mobilize the whole Church to work for the Kingdom of God. They are a great unifying force. The people need to hear the Church's prophetic word in favor of peace and justice.

The Christian base communities are small, like the mustard seed. But when planted in fertile soil, they make the Church grow like a leafy tree. Although they do not have the power of great institutions, they have the power of the Gospel. *August 1983*

IF YOU HAD FAITH THE SIZE OF A MUSTARD SEED, YOU COULD SAY TO THE SYCAMORE, "BE UPROOTED AND TRANSPLANTED INTO THE SEA," AND IT WOULD OBEY YOU.

LUKE 17:6

A PRIEST'S RECOLLECTION OF A VISIT TO AN ORPHANAGE

JUANITO'S FIRST CONFESSION

The destruction of human life during ten years of war and repression cannot be measured. Psychological trauma and stolen childhoods are not statistics. Thousands of children have been left orphans by the war. Many more have witnessed the slaughter of a mother or father. In this selection, a priest shares his reflections after visiting an orphanage.

The orphanage is on a hill overlooking San Salvador. The view of the city is beautiful, especially at this time of year when the grass is green and flowers are everywhere. As in other parts of the country affected by the war, this natural beauty contrasts with the children's pain.

The home is for children who are victims of the war. The parents of some of the children have been killed. The parents of other children are political prisoners or are in the war zones. I have just returned from hearing the children's confessions.

The children have suffered terribly. Some of them were forced to witness their parents, brothers and sisters being beaten, raped or hacked to pieces with machetes. Now they suffer from lack of appetite, neurosis, depression and insomnia.

One 13-year-old girl was raped and then forced to witness the torture and killing of her mother and brothers. "She became ill," the psychologist who treated her said. "Not physically ill, but ill from sadness. Shortly afterwards she died. I had never seen anyone die of sadness before."

I will never forget an eleven-year-old boy named Juanito whom I met at this orphanage. A few years ago, he was found beneath the bullet-riddled bodies of his mother, grandmother and three older brothers. Juanito was covered with blood, but unharmed. The other survivors of this massacre brought Juanito and his sisters to the orphanage. According to his sisters, Juanito tries to keep his spirits up, but he still spends entire days totally withdrawn, without speaking a word to anyone.

After his confession, Juanito put his hand on my shoulder, looked me in the eye and said, "Father, pray for me, so that I can forgive the soldiers who killed my mother and brothers. I do not want to live with hatred in my heart." *January 1985*

FORGIVE WHATEVER GRIEVANCES YOU HAVE AGAINST ONE ANOTHER. FORGIVE AS THE LORD HAS FORGIVEN YOU.

COLOSSIANS 3:13

A STORY OF COMPASSION

NO ROOM IN THE REFUGE

One out of every four Salvadorans has been displaced by the war. More than 500,000 people have crowded into the cities, particularly San Salvador. In the early 1980s, many—like the people in this story—found refuge in churches, retreat houses or the Archdiocesan seminary.

A few days ago, in the early morning hours, forty people from the countryside— mostly children and a few women and elderly people—arrived at a refuge for displaced persons. They had walked for several days, fleeing the bombings. They arrived barefoot, dirty and tired from the long journey. Nervous but relieved, they knocked on the door. At last, they thought, they had found safety.

But the doorkeeper, a displaced person himself, had to tell them that there was no room. The camp was overcrowded.

The people did not understand. They pleaded, telling the doorkeeper that they had left everything behind and did not know anyone in the city. They had nowhere else to go. Exhausted and afraid, they begged to enter. They asked, "How can you leave us in the street?"

The doorkeeper let them in. "God knows where we will find room, but we cannot turn you away," he said.

Those already in the refuge received the new arrivals warmly. They, too, had passed through this moment of crisis. They knew what it meant to finally reach sanctuary.

Later in the morning, the community leaders in the camp met with the new arrivals to offer whatever help they could. They prayed to God for consolation and encouragement. After a few minutes the exhausted children fell asleep, the first time in days that they had slept safe from bombs and bullets. They slept peacefully, as children should always sleep.

In the refuge the meeting continued, but the question on everyone's mind was, "What will happen if others come? There is no more room."   *August 1985*

LOOK ON THE NEEDS OF THE SAINTS AS YOUR OWN; BE GENEROUS IN OFFERING HOSPITALITY.

ROMANS 12:13

Free the Oppressed

| THE STORY OF A PERSECUTED CHURCH

"DO NOT FEAR! PREACH THE GOOD NEWS!"

Resurrection Lutheran Church in San Salvador has been bombed several times. Its pastor, Bishop Medardo Gómez, was tortured several years ago, and has often been threatened with death. This selection was written in December 1988, a few days after the second bombing of the church offices. Since then, the attacks have continued. The church was bombed a third time in May 1989, and in November of the same year, fifteen churchworkers, among them twelve internationals, were captured by the National Guard.

The day after Christmas, at three o'clock in the morning, a group of armed men broke into Resurrection Lutheran Church. They knocked the cross from the altar and ransacked the church. When they left, they set off a powerful bomb destroying the church offices. There were no injuries, but the damage was extensive.

The persecution of the Lutheran Church continues. Several members of the Church have been captured. The office has been repeatedly burglarized and raided. Bombs have exploded at the children's home run by the Lutheran Church, and Bishop Medardo Gómez has received many death threats.

"They call us subversives," commented Bishop Gómez. "But the truth is that the Lutheran Church in El Salvador is effectively living its option for the poor. The Church is well known for supporting the dialogue between the government and the FMLN guerrillas. For example, we participate in the National Debate for Peace, and we have publicly stated our position. The Lutheran Church has become an active Christian protagonist in the midst of the tragedy of El Salvador."

Bishop Medardo's reaction to the attack was clear. He called for an investigation and demanded that the attacks against his Church and against the poor cease. He also pardoned those who committed the attack. Above all, he promised that the Lutheran Church would continue its ecclesial option for the poor.

Two days later, on December 28, the sanctuary of Resurrection Church was filled with supporters of many faiths in a gesture of ecumenical solidarity. On the altar stood the crucifix that had been desecrated. Just as Christ proclaimed two thousand years ago, the message of the service was, "Do not fear, but preach the good news to the poor. Remember, 'Blessed are you when they persecute you for my sake.'"
December 1988

GO INTO THE WHOLE WORLD AND PROCLAIM THE GOOD NEWS TO ALL CREATION.
MARK 16:15

A PRIEST'S RECOLLECTION OF HOLY WEEK

ARISING FROM THE ASHES

Guarjila and many other villages in the Department of Chalatenango were forcibly depopulated by the Armed Forces' bombing and ground incursions in the early 1980s. Most of the survivors fled and sought refuge in camps in Honduras. Seven years later, the refugees organized a repatriation to repopulate their abandoned homes in El Salvador. In the following selection, a North American priest writes about his visit to Guarjila during Holy Week in 1988.

The village of Guarjila is hidden in a valley between the mountains. The hills were burned recently by the Army to deprive the guerrillas of any cover. At the beginning of Holy Week, soldiers occupied the village. On Good Friday, we heard eight bombs explode nearby.

On Holy Saturday we met in an open field in the light of a full moon and celebrated the coming of Easter. For hundreds of those present, it was the first Holy Week they had celebrated in their country since fleeing to Honduras as refugees, seven years earlier.

On this day, the people worked on a sad but sacred task. On small pieces of paper they wrote the names of all their family members and friends who had been murdered during seven years of war. The list of one woman's dead relatives did not fit on her paper. One man, Rafael, said a prayer for the eleven members of his family who had been murdered by the death squads.

In the evening a thousand of us gathered around the fire which would light the Easter candle. By the light of the fire, I saw the faces of young people, of mothers weary from the day's work, and of elderly people who had survived the hardships of war and exile. Many people spoke about the meaning of the Easter candle, and I realized that they expected me to share a few words.

How was I to explain what their lists of murdered loved ones meant to me? What could I say in response to their tremendous suffering and the many deaths and massacres they had endured? The only reason I felt I could say anything was because, looking at their faces, I saw their hope.

In the six months since their return to El Salvador, a thousand men and women have created a community. They have built homes and planted fields. Out of chaos and death, they have created life.

I also remembered what I had seen that morning. We had walked to San Antonio de los Ranchos, a small community hidden in the hills of Chalatenango. The day before, a battle had taken place between the Army and the guerrillas. The village looked like a ghost town. The church had been bombed, houses were destroyed, and the plaza had been turned into rubble. Many other small villages suffer the same violence.

This is the fundamental mystery of Christianity—the emergence of life from death. The people understand this mystery.

Perhaps some light can be shed on this by describing what happened on Holy Thursday. On this day the Church commemorates the Christian commandment to love and serve one another in the washing of the feet. Here in Guarjila, however, the people used another symbol. An old man gave a young widow an armful of firewood, and she gave him some *tortillas*. These gestures expressed service to one another. This new symbol of firewood and *tortillas* added an important element: the mutuality of service and the giving and taking which builds community.

This is how they expressed their faith: To go from death to life is to grow from individualism to community. These people who pray for their dead, also pray for their oppressors. We prayed for their 3,000 murdered family members and also for the soldiers who committed these crimes. Then one woman said, "May we always be able to love, to hope and to forgive."

During this Holy Week, I became convinced that sharing is a great truth that cannot be concealed. The oppressors will not triumph over the victims, just as they did not triumph over Jesus. From Guarjila, a thousand men, women and children proclaim to the world that they have not been vanquished. They proclaim a new way to live, oriented toward community service, work and hope. They speak of a new way to die and of resurrection. *June 1988*

WHY DO YOU SEARCH FOR THE LIVING AMONG THE DEAD? HE IS NOT HERE; HE HAS BEEN RAISED UP.

LUKE 24:5B,6A

A LETTER TO HIS BISHOP

A PRIEST'S DECISION

Like many Salvadoran Christians, Father Rutilio Sánchez has reflected on his commitment to serve the poor in a society characterized by gross social injustice. In 1982, after long deliberation, he decided to go to the Department of Chalatenango and carry out his pastoral ministry in an area controlled by the FMLN guerrillas. He wrote this letter from a war zone. It was addressed to Archbishop Rivera y Damas and "Christian friends and people of good will."

I believe the time has come to take another step forward in my life. I have received beautiful gifts from God, but the greatest gift has been the opportunity to serve my people at this time when they are making great sacrifices. To honor the memory of so many martyrs, I must live my love for my Salvadoran brothers and sisters each day.

I believe that priesthood is a commitment to serve the community. I believe Jesus Christ as he is present in the people who teach us how to transform this cruel society into a loving one. As his disciple have decided not to abandon this sacrament but to make it prophetic, accompanying the Christian communities of El Salvador.

The pastoral needs in the area where am going are great: consoling those who are grieving, hearing confession and giving communion to those who are dying, and teaching catechism to the many orphaned children. The suffering of the people living in these valleys and mountains calls us to commit ourselves to struggle for liberation.

I will accompany these sheep who are without a shepherd. Their hearts and souls need the strength of the Lord's Supper. Many young children have not been baptized and I want to be with them. This struggle will not be won just with bullets; the commitment of Christians is also necessary. I will try to fulfill the words of the Apostle Paul which are on my seal of

> I want only to take up the cross and follow Jesus in the ravines, the hills and the trenches where the Kingdom of God is being fulfilled.

ordination: "A priest is called from the people to serve the people."

I will teach literacy, care for the sick, carry the wounded. Shacks and caves will serve as chapels where we will celebrate the Eucharist and the Resurrection of the carpenter of Nazareth.

I want only to take up the cross and follow Jesus in the ravines, the hills and the trenches where the Kingdom of God is being fulfilled, in which there will be enough bread for everyone, and our people will not die young.

As a priest, as one who seeks a greater faithfulness to the Gospel, and as a brother who wants to be responsible to his people, I say with joy: Until we meet again, my greeting and embrace be with you.

Father José Rutilio Sánchez   June 1982

OUR DESIRE IS THAT EACH OF YOU SHOW THE SAME ZEAL TO THE END, FULLY ASSURED OF THAT FOR WHICH YOU HOPE. DO NOT GROW LAZY, BUT IMITATE THOSE WHO, THROUGH FAITH AND PATIENCE, ARE INHERITING THE PROMISES

HEBREWS 6:11-12

| DIARY EXCERPT OF A PRIEST IN A WAR ZONE

HOW THE CHILDREN PLAY

Father Rutilio Sánchez, who wrote the previous letter, described the faith of the people in the midst of war in the Department of Chalatenango.

My pastoral work in Chalatenango gives me a vision of the future. Here we are living in a way that, God willing, all Christians will be able to live someday. People work together and the spirit of the community

DURING EACH ARMY INVASION, THE SOLDIERS BURN DOWN THE LITTLE SHELTERS AND SHACKS THAT SERVE AS CLASSROOMS.

grows every day. Food is shared in the village, regardless of how scarce it is. Alcohol has been outlawed and there is little crime.

Still, we have difficulties. One of the most serious is the education of our children. During each Army invasion, the soldiers burn down the little shelters and shacks which serve as classrooms. We have very few pencils, notebooks or schoolbooks. The children do not have enough paper to practice writing. But they are

creative. They write with charcoal on of wood rather than with pencils and

Despite war, children always play lack toys, but not imagination. They u little pieces of wood for oxen to pull a or a plow. The children pretend to for caravan bringing supplies. Clever at i tion, they also pretend to fight the wa reenacting ambushes, occupations of villages, invasions, searches and bon They take prisoners of war and treat "with respect for their human rights, v doing to them what the enemy Army d They take care of the "prisoners," tre their wounds and then releasing them people's side always wins in these ga

The war has made the children ol their years. Their questions are devas "If the FMLN has mercy on its enemie do the government troops show no me when they invade our villages?"

In the afternoons the communitie full of playing children. They stop playi and react quickly when the A-37's fly overhead. I don't know how they can h the planes over the noise of their gam but they hear them before the adults d They build their own shelters from the bombs and then play in them. Sometin envy how happy they are in the middle this war.

We teach three levels of catechism classes for the children. The youngest children learn to say prayers and to understand their meaning and history. In the second class they learn the 10 Commandments, the 14 Works of Mercy and the 8 Beatitudes. In the third class we discuss the sacraments and the Gospel parables.

Before I came, many of the people had not seen a priest for three years. When I arrived they told me that there had not been a Mass since Archbishop Romero was assassinated.

Every community has a catechist. Pastoral work in all the communities is coordinated, usually within the official parish boundaries. I am the only priest in the whole area of Guazapa and Chalatenango. I walk to the outlying communities to be with the sick and to celebrate Mass. The Holy Spirit accompanies us. Like the people of Israel, we in El Salvador are writing a great Bible. Life here is on a large scale: great sadness, great joy, military invasions and hunger. But we are accompanied by great heroes who defend our communities. Above all, we are accompanied by a great faith which keeps us from becoming insensitive to death. We are called to struggle for life and for the future when there will be greater possibili-

ties for realizing the Kingdom of God and when the 10 Commandments, the 14 Works of Mercy and the 8 Beatitudes will become a reality. *January 1983*

THE HARVEST IS GOOD BUT LABORERS ARE SCARCE. BEG THE HARVEST MASTER TO SEND OUT LABORERS TO GATHER HIS HARVEST.
MATTHEW 9:37B-38

A LETTER TO THE CHURCHES OF THE WORLD

WRITING A NEW TESTAMENT IN CHALATENANGO

The following letter was written by the Christian communities in the war zones and sent to the Oscar Romero Pastoral Center in San Salvador.

The Christian communities of Chalatenango, Aguilares, Guazapa, Suchitoto, Cinquera and Tejutepeque send you their greetings and thank you for accompanying us. A New Testament is being written in El Salvador, based on the experiences of our people. May our greeting reach all people of good will and all Churches in the world.

We decided to write you to assure you that Christianity is alive in these areas controlled by the FMLN and that our faith motivates us to work for peace in our communities. The nightmare of persecution which you in the cities suffer—because of your commitment to announce the Gospel and denounce injustice—is not present here. We do, however, suffer the war.

We are forced to create a new way of life in the midst of mortars, bombings and Army invasions which destroy everything. We have a strong sense of cooperation. A loving Christian community gives us strength in the face of so much violence—the result of the U.S. weapons which have inundated our country.

Although it is dangerous for you to acknowledge us by name—because of the government persecution—be assured that we Christians are present here, growing food, working in health and education, and caring for each other. We have children and schools, and we protect our hospitals and elderly people during the Army invasions which seek to exterminate even the weakest.

We want to be in communion with the Church. In the absence of priests, we have overcome our isolation through the work of the catechists who visit and encourage our communities.

We identify with the history of those who confronted the Roman Empire and grew stronger when Rome tried to destroy a newborn Christianity. We believe that neither Herod nor Pilate will be able to destroy the children of God who desire peace and justice and who make possible the advent of the Kingdom of God.

Christ was reborn in our midst this past Christmas. Our children identify with the child who was born in a manger, as we identify with Mary and Joseph.   *April 1983*

ON THE LORD'S DAY I WAS CAUGHT UP IN ECSTASY AND I HEARD BEHIND ME A PIERCING VOICE LIKE THE SOUND OF A TRUMPET, WHICH SAID, "WRITE ON A SCROLL WHAT YOU NOW SEE AND SEND IT TO THE SEVEN CHURCHES."

REVELATION 1:10

THE TESTIMONY OF A PRIEST IN A WAR ZONE

THE CHURCH OF THE POOR IN MORAZAN

In the following account a Salvadoran priest, Father Miguel Ventura, describes the contribution of Christians to the process of structural change. He works north of the Torola River in the Department of Morazán, a stronghold of the FMLN guerrillas.

For the last twenty years we have been engaged in a liberation struggle in El Salvador. This struggle grew out of our awareness of the need to transform unjust structures in our society. In this transformation, a new model of Church is being born. We call unjust structures "sinful" because they go against the will of God; it is against these structures that we must struggle. Not only a new model of society, but a new model of being Christian and of being Church is at stake.

As Christians in Morazán, we have gained a greater understanding of the specific contribution of the Church to the struggle for liberation. I believe we have achieved a great deal of freedom to pursue our pastoral mission. The pastoral teams function in all the communities. We are able to celebrate the religious feast days, the sacraments, the Mass and every other Christian ritual. Many public and prophetic activities are Christian in nature: vigils, fasts, processions for justice and peace.

One of the fundamental and specifically Christian contributions to the struggle for liberation is to offer a critical attitude. There is no reason for our faith to be subordinated to any political project; nor can a political project succeed if it imposes itself on the religious beliefs of the people. We have learned how to live our faith in a situation of structural change. We dialogue with the FMLN leaders to help them remain worthy of the people's trust.

Our Christian faith also makes an important contribution by giving hope to people in such difficult moments. How is it possible that after nine years of war and 70,000 deaths, our people still hope and have a vision for the future? I believe that it is our Christian faith which gives them hope.

For this reason, I believe that it would be a great mistake for the Church not to get involved in the struggle for liberation. The Church itself can learn a lot, and it can contribute something important: constructive criticism and hope for the future.

May 1989

ELIJAH APPEALED TO ALL THE PEOPLE AND SAID, "HOW LONG WILL YOU STRADDLE THE ISSUE? IF THE LORD IS GOD, FOLLOW THE LORD; IF BAAL, FOLLOW BAAL."

I KINGS 18:21A

A TESTIMONY FROM A REPOPULATED COMMUNITY

WAITING FOR THE HARVEST

Arcatao is in the northern part of the Department of Chalatenango, the heart of one of the war zones, close to the border with Honduras. Frequent bombings, strafings and Army incursions are a fact of life in Arcatao. It is one of the few villages in the area that was never completely abandoned. During the past two years, those who have returned have rebuilt their homes and planted their fields. In this testimony, a campesino who returned to Arcatao describes his hope for the future.

It had been seven years since the military destroyed our village. I was the first to return with my family. When I saw the little house where I grew up, I felt anxious. I went inside and began to repair some of the damage, cutting branches to cover the holes in the roof. After the house had been cleaned and repaired, it looked nice and we got up enough courage to begin life anew.

I went walking in the mountains around the village and found five families living nearby. All of them said that they preferred to die in the village, whether they were killed by one side or the other, rather than leave.

The Army had told the people that the "subversives" might come to the village and kill everyone they found there. So when the people saw armed men and women arrive, they were very frightened. But when the

guerrillas approached and greeted them i a friendly manner, the people began to ta with them and to feel safer. When the guerrillas left, they told the people, "You have nothing to fear from us. Work in peace."

The people thanked God. Now they s that they are more afraid of the governm Army, and that the soldiers are much wo than the guerrillas.

When other people found out we ha returned, the idea spread, and many pe took courage to do the same. Today the are 150 families in Arcatao and more ar coming. We have become a community again and hold regular meetings. We are looking for volunteers to teach both the children and the adults. We wrote to Monsignor Rivera y Damas asking for a pastoral team to come here. They come although only once or twice a month. Bu we are accomplishing a lot.

We have had to endure still more cruelty from the Army. Our only sin is ha returned to our little village, which we lo so much. They have killed some of us w were brave enough to return here. Other have been tortured. The Army steals ou food which we carry on our backs from Guarjila, fifteen miles away. In ten minu they take our food to their barracks by helicopter, while it takes us two days of walking to bring it to our village. The whole time we are in constant danger of the military bombing or machine-gunning us.

A curse on the men who invented those planes for the destruction of humanity. May the men who invented planes for the service of humanity be blessed.

We are ordinary people who must work constantly to support our children. Now we have learned how to improve our community, and we want the military to leave us in peace. We want to watch our fields of corn grow and see stalks of corn bend in the wind. We feel so happy when we walk through a field of corn and listen to the rustle of the green leaves, but we must also protect the field from the insects which try to destroy it. How beautiful it is to see the pink, purple and white flowers of the bean plants! Each dawn we touch the drops of precious dew on their leaves, and we know that the fields are being transformed into an abundance of food that will feed the community.

The children shout with joy when they see their fathers return from the fields carrying bundles of bean plants on their shoulders. They begin to shell the beans and to sing songs. As parents whose children have often gone hungry, we understand their joy at the sight of food.

We still need to get a doctor and medicines, and we do not know how to go about this. People may die when there is no medicine. It is possible that there is a doctor who wants to work with us, but the government won't allow him to come here. It is as though this were a foreign country where special documents are necessary to travel. Nor do we have the necessary identification to leave our village. Some people went to the town of Chalatenango to see if the officials would give us documents, but they returned worse off than when they left because now they are even more afraid. No one gets identification papers. It is as if we were less than human.

On August 24 we will celebrate the day of our patron saint, Saint Bartholomew. Our village has always celebrated this festival, but this will be the biggest celebration since the war began. We are going forward!
July 1987

YOU SHALL KEEP THE FEAST OF THE HAR-VEST, OF THE FIRST FRUITS OF YOUR LABOR, OF WHAT YOU SOW IN THE FIELD. YOU SHALL KEEP THE FEAST OF INGATHERING AT THE END OF THE YEAR, WHEN YOU GATHER IN FROM THE FIELD THE FRUIT OF YOUR LABOR.
EXODUS 23:16

A SPRING WHOSE WATERS NEVER RUN DRY

On March 18, 1981, the people of Santa Marta, in the Department of Cabañas, were forced to abandon their homes. Five thousand men, women and children crossed the Lempa River into Honduras under fire from both the Salvadoran and Honduran Armies. Dozens drowned or were shot. Six years later, 1,100 refugees returned to their homes in Santa Marta from the refugee camp in Mesa Grande, Honduras. A Protestant pastor recorded the following dialogue.

When the refugees from Mesa Grande arrived here, they celebrated their hope and their commitment to each other by giving thanks to God. The reading they chose for the occasion was a beautiful text from the prophet Isaiah, written after the return of the People of Israel from exile.

The catechist gathered the people, inviting them to sit on the grassy field. After a short introduction, there was a dialogue between the catechist and the people based on the text from Isaiah:

"God will always guide you," the catechist began.

"Yes, yes!" an old man responded. "It is true, the Lord is the one who called us and guided our return. God has helped us."

"And you shall be like a watered garden."

"Yes, brothers and sisters," said a woman, "we will build a new society, different from before. It used to be everyone for himself; now we are learning how to work together. If we only trust in God, we can live out a miracle, and all of us will have enough corn to eat, a new society, a new way of working and a new way of living."

The catechist reminded the people of how important it is to live like this, and how such a life requires courage and faith.

The dialogue continued; "A spring whose waters never run dry."

Several people commented, and then the catechist added, "We are called to build a new society. As Salvadorans, we must be a light to all nations. We must help break the chains that enslave our brothers and sisters in other countries. They are living the same situation as we are. This is the spring which never runs dry: the Word of God and the building of a new society in El Salvador. We must be in solidarity with the people of other nations, so that all people may be free."

The celebration ended with these words: "You will rebuild the ancient ruins and build up the old foundations."

At this point their words cease to be commentary. The explanation of the Word of God is not just symbolic or personal—it is quite literal. You can still see the ruins of what were once their houses, destroyed by the Army.

As the reflection came to an end, a man said, "We are going to build our new homes on the ruins of our burnt-out houses."

The celebration of the Word has ended, as has their exile. A new life awaits them.
November 1987

"GOD WILL ALWAYS GUIDE YOU, GIVING YOU RELIEF IN DESERT PLACES. GOD WILL GIVE STRENGTH TO YOUR BONES, AND YOU SHALL BE LIKE A WATERED GARDEN, LIKE A SPRING WHOSE WATERS NEVER RUN DRY.
ISAIAH 58:11

A LITURGY IN A REPOPULATED COMMUNITY

A RUSTY CHALICE

The community of Copapayo, in the Department of Cuscatlán, has suffered a succession of massacres. On November 4, 1983, 118 people were slaughtered by the Atlacatl Battalion, an elite Army unit trained by the U.S. military. The survivors sought refuge in Honduras, and by 1985 the entire region had become a free-fire zone.

The first repopulation of Copapayo involved the return of 700 refugees from Mesa Grande, Honduras, in October 1987. Their return to their homes in the war zones has not been easy, but the former refugees say that with their new skills and a new model of community life, they can contribute to bringing peace to El Salvador. A North American churchworker who visited Copapayo shared this account.

Today, November 7, is a special day. The priest and the pastoral team came from the refugee camp of Mesa Grande to celebrate Mass. The Mass celebrated the people's return, and they hoped that it would motivate those who still remained in Mesa Grande to come back.

The priest began the celebration with these words: "We lift up this chalice, buried four years ago with the church bells here in Copapayo, as a symbol of the suffering of our people mixed with the blood of Christ. We celebrate this Mass in commemoration of your suffering, your history, your desire to return and your presence here."

"These *tortillas* are our daily bread, consecrated by God, just as we are called to consecrate each day of our lives to the Lord."

This Mass was special—and ordinary—joining the daily suffering of the poor with the Bread of Life, mixing the blood of their martyrs with the blood of Christ. It lifted up the cup of salvation—a little rusty now—with the invincible determination of this people to begin a new life in their own land. The struggle continues for a day when justice, peace and freedom will reign in El Salvador.

The Army still spreads terror among the population, but the people have not lost their faith or courage. The blood of their martyrs has become the seed of new Christians. In small gestures and in their daily work there are signs in Copapayo that the poor are building a just and dignified life in El Salvador.   *December 1987*

WHEN THE LORD BROUGHT BACK THE CAPTIVES OF ZION, IT WAS AS IF WE WERE DREAMING. THEN OUR MOUTH WAS FILLED WITH LAUGHTER AND OUR TONGUE WITH REJOICING.

PSALMS 126:1

A STORY OF POPULAR PROTEST

THE MARCH FOR PEACE

The National Debate for Peace was formed in September 1988. It is a coalition of more than 80 labor and farmworker federations, cooperatives, professional associations, churches, universities and associations of small and medium-sized businesses. The organizations participating in the National Debate have forged a common agenda for peace, calling for dialogue and political negotiation among the government, the FMLN and all social sectors. They have organized several marches for peace, one of which is described below.

On Saturday, March 4, 1989 the National Debate organized a march for peace, the second in the last few months. Twenty thousand men, women, and children marched. They walked with palm branches symbolizing peace and carried the blue-and-white colors of the Salvadoran flag. The march expressed the commitment of the Salvadoran people to achieve peace. Thousands of spectators observed from the sidewalks, expressing sympathy with the march.

The shouts and the speeches in Parque Libertad called for a peace that is achieved not through violence, but through dialogue and negotiations. They called for peace with justice and dignity. Bishop Medardo Gómez of the Lutheran Church of El Salvador said, "We remember the situation of God's people living under oppression in Egypt and God's covenant with them. We long for a Promised Land in El Salvador with work, housing, health, education and security for all."

The rector of the Central American University (UCA), Father Ignacio Ellacuría, spoke next. "Peace should not be left in the hands of those for whom party interests are more important than the needs of the people, but should be in the hands of those who truly long for peace.

"We need to work for peace from the perspective of the suffering of the orphans and widows, and the tragedy of the assassinated and disappeared. We must keep our eyes on the God of Jesus Christ, the God of life, the God of the poor, and not on the idols or the gods of death that devour everything."

El Salvador cries out for peace. The 70,000 dead. The 7,000 disappeared. The widows and orphans. The one and one-half million displaced people and refugees and the millions of impoverished Salvadorans. How many more?   *March 1989*

EVERY NATION DIVIDED AGAINST ITSELF IS LAID WASTE; ANY HOUSE TORN BY DISSENTION FALLS.

LUKE 11:17

A STORY OF SOLIDARITY

THE FAST OF THE POOR

In El Salvador "solidarity" has become synonymous with international efforts to respond to the urgent needs of the poor and to the cause of justice. But solidarity is also offered by one poor community to another. The following account by a visitor to a displaced persons camp recounts the sacrifice of people who remember loved ones still in a war zone.

News recently came to the people in a displaced persons camp that their relatives who are still living in a war zone had suffered terribly from a recent military operation. They called a meeting to discuss what they could do. One person proposed that the whole camp fast for a day. Everyone agreed. The food they saved would be sent to the villagers who had suffered at the hands of the Army.

On the day of the fast, everyone was smiling. They worked as usual in the communal kitchen, the clinic and the school. A young woman recalled, "Jesus said that when we fast we should let our faces shine."

We asked them why they were fasting. A 12-year-old boy said, "We want to share the pain of our brothers and sisters who are hungry. We want to help with what little we have, so that everyone might eat."

As we were leaving, we asked them what they wanted to say to people who would hear the story of their fast. Without hesitation one woman said, "We would like you to know that we fast so that everyone might be strengthened. We fast to share the suffering of our brothers and sisters who hunger for justice as well as for food. We support them, and we ask you to support them as well."

An elderly man added, "We are not just fasting. God willing, we will send our food to our friends and relatives who are suffering."

These people, already displaced by the war, are like the widow in the Gospel who gave her last penny.   *July 1983*

THIS, RATHER, IS THE FAST THAT I WISH: TO SHARE YOUR BREAD WITH THE HUNGRY, TO SHELTER THE OPPRESSED AND THE HOMELESS.
ISAIAH 58:6A,7A

e fast to
are the
ffering of
r brothers
d sisters
ho hunger
r justice

THE STORY OF A CHRISTIAN COMMUNITY

ON THE ROAD TO JERICHO

Government security forces in El Salvador capture approximately two hundred civilians every week. They are accused of collaborating with organizations that the government considers subversive. If no one witnesses the capture and identifies the security forces responsible, the captured person may "be disappeared." Those who denounce the capture of a loved one risk the same fate.

In this story a community in the countryside faces this situation.

A young man was traveling from his village to San Salvador to arrange permission for a water project. He was captured by the security forces in a bus station. As soon as his family found out, they went to the priest to read the parable of the Good Samaritan. After listening to the parable, a member of the community stood and said, "All of us are afraid to say or do anything for people who are captured. We have come to Mass because we are Christians. The Word of God says that we have to show our love through actions.

"The military says that the people they captured sell food to the guerrillas. But these people are like the man who was beaten and left lying on the road. We do not try to help those captured because we are afraid. But the Lord tells us to love each other as we love ourselves. I ask myself: If tomorrow I were captured, what would I want my brothers and sisters to do?"

At the end of the Mass, the priest

ALL OF US ARE AFRAID TO SAY OR DO ANYTHING FOR PEOPLE WHO ARE CAPTURED...THE WORD OF GOD SAYS THAT WE HAVE TO SHOW OUR LOVE THROUGH ACTIONS

military barracks to appeal for his release, but without results. Two days later, his wife and their six-year-old daughter were also captured.

This led the community to take action. During Mass that day, the people asked the asked that those who were interested in this problem stay for a meeting. Everyone stayed, but they were subdued and silent. Finally one person spoke. "If anyone says anything, the next day that person could be the one captured."

One of the women said quietly to her husband, "Luis, don't be a coward. Say something."

After a pause, Luis, half mumbling his words, said, "I think there are some of us who could go tomorrow to the military barracks to ask why they are holding the people who were captured. We could testify that they are good people. I think we should sign up and go together."

The women were the first to sign their names. Although they were afraid, they committed themselves to go to the military barracks to protest. One woman said, "The Holy Virgin knows that we are not going to

do anything that is wrong and she will protect us."

In spite of their fear, twelve people volunteered to petition the military for the family's release. To give themselves more courage they prayed a rosary that night.
February 1987

"WHICH OF THESE THREE, IN YOUR OPINION, WAS NEIGHBOR TO THE MAN WHO FELL IN WITH THE ROBBERS?" THE ANSWER CAME, "THE ONE WHO TREATED HIM WITH COMPASSION." JESUS SAID TO HIM, "THEN GO AND DO THE SAME."

LUKE 10:36-37

A LETTER OF SOLIDARITY FROM A WAR ZONE

EARTHQUAKE IN SAN SALVADOR

On October 10, 1986, a major earthquake struck San Salvador, leaving 200,000 people homeless. In the days following the earthquake, people in the poor neighborhoods organized committees for food distribution, health care and emergency shelter. The degree of participation of the poor in relief efforts astonished international observers. The community organizations created in those first days are still strong and active today.

Both the reflection and the letter below show the solidarity of the poor in the war zones with the earthquake victims.

There is no doubt that the earthquake has been a profound religious experience for the Salvadoran people and that God has been present to them during this time. Three responses of the faith community to this tragedy stand out. One has been to thank God for life and for the survival of one's family. Another has been to interpret the earthquake as a punishment for the nation's sins. A third response has been to see the earthquake as a powerful call from God for conversion to justice, peace and solidarity.

There have been many acts of solidarity. Doctors and nurses have spent countless hours treating the wounded. Many privileged young people—perhaps for the first time in their lives—have come into contact with the real situation of San Salvador as they bring water, food and medicine to shacks in the poor shantytowns.

People from all walks of life ask, "How can we help?" For a few moments, solidarity is present in a country divided by the war and leveled by destruction. Teachers and students, professionals and the poor, priests and laborers work together. The guerrillas have declared a cease-fire, and even some of the soldiers have helped to clear away the rubble.

The people who live north of the Torola River in the Department of Morazán live in extreme poverty in an area affected by the war. Yet they have shown their solidarity with the victims of the earthquake. On November 6, 1986, seven truckloads of fruit and lumber arrived at the Archdiocese of San Salvador. The trucks came from Perquín, Nahuaterique, Zancudo, Los Patios, San Fernando, Torola and San Diego. One of the trucks carried forty wooden posts made by children in a school in Perquín. With the supplies was a letter to the earthquake victims.

Dear brothers and sisters in San Salvador:

As you suffer during these difficult days, the people living north of the Torola

River in Morazán want to tell you that we understand what it is to lose a loved one, to lose a home, to be injured, and to be left without work. You have had to live this cruel reality during the last few days. We have lived it for six years, victims of another "earthquake"—the war. Bombs, mortars, bullets and fire have destroyed thousands of human lives and left thousands more wounded. Our houses, forests and crops have been destroyed. Like you, many of us have been displaced from our homes.

But the suffering caused by the war has not destroyed our love, our solidarity or our hope. We derive strength from our poverty, in order to bring you the fruits of the land which—despite the destruction— still produces food and timber. We bring you the fruits of our labor as well. Though we have endured every trial and sacrifice, we are still able to offer our solidarity.

We realize that our contribution is not great, but it expresses what we have learned from our difficult experience. We can survive any trial or sacrifice when we give—not only from abundance, but from our poverty. Together with this fruit and lumber, we send you a message of hope and strength. These words are not something we say easily. They come from our life which is filled with difficult trials.

The suffering caused by the war, which has gone on for six years, has caused many to lose hope. Some have fled; others have died. But in the midst of these trials we have discovered that there is only one way to survive—to extend our love, our collaboration and our friendship to others.

Our words of hope are these: We can survive any adversity if we stand together. If this is the hour of trial, it is also our hour of solidarity. We trust in each other and in God. Suffering has brought us closer to you, and suffering has called us to walk together. *October/November 1986*

IF ONE PART OF THE BODY SUFFERS, EVERY PART SUFFERS WITH IT; IF ONE PART IS HONORED, EVERY PART REJOICES WITH IT. NOW YOU ARE THE BODY OF CHRIST
1 CORINTHIANS 12:26-27A

A TESTIMONY OF ORGANIZED WOMEN

FOR THE SAKE OF PEACE... WOMEN, ORGANIZE!

In El Salvador women have suffered particularly from the grinding poverty which denies health, education and decent employment to them and their loved ones. Poverty and repression have disintegrated families and, in the poorest communities, women head most households. During the past decade, women have organized to better understand and struggle against their exploitation.

On August 14, 1988, poor women from all over the country gathered in San Salvador at the first Assembly of Marginalized Women and discussed the needs of their families. The following selection is a report of that gathering.

"We marginalized women share many of the same problems, and if we organize, we can overcome them." So said Imelda, a woman from a shantytown on the edge of San Salvador.

The atmosphere in the auditorium where the Assembly met was charged with expectation and hope. One woman called out a refrain as the others responded in chorus:

"Organized women... will never be evicted!"

"Our response to inequality... is more unity!"

"For the sake of peace... women, organize!"

"What do we want for our children?... Schools, not barracks!"

The assembly heard many speeches about the urgent needs felt by these women. Their concerns are shared by women everywhere.

Lack of adequate housing: "Our houses are shacks built with discarded tin, cardboard, plastic or other junk. Some of us live in one small room made of mud and sticks. We have to wrap our children in plastic so that they won't get wet. Our shacks are next to rivers filled with sewage. We live with the fear that the rains will carry our homes and children away. Some of us live along the railroad tracks. We are always afraid that a train will run over and kill our children. Some of us live on steep hillsides where there is a danger of being buried in a landslide."

Lack of employment: "We almost never have steady work. When we find work we are paid extremely low wages. Often the

---

SOME OF US LIVE IN ONE SMALL ROOM MADE OF MUD AND STICKS. WE HAVE TO WRAP OUR CHILDREN IN PLASTIC SO THAT THEY WON'T GET WET.

---

bosses do not respect us and take advantage of us. We do whatever work we can find. We sell fruit, vegetables, newspapers or bottles. Our children are often left without care during the day."

Inadequate health care: "The health of our families deteriorates every day. We cannot pay private doctors because we barely have enough money to survive."

Poor nutrition: "Nutrition is always poor because our low wages do not permit us to buy enough food. The rising cost of basic foods has made this situation even worse.

Many of our families survive by picking through the garbage for food. Others have resigned themselves to waking up and going to bed hungry."

Forced military recruitment: "The government, instead of searching for a solution to these problems, forces our children into military service. Our sons are victims of the war. They do not even know why they are fighting or why they die. Sometimes our sons return alive, but many return only to be buried. Then the government gives us a medal, as though this could replace our sons."

These women organized themselves because they are convinced that nobody else will do anything for them. The first Assembly of Marginalized Women is a sign of hope.   *September 1988*

SHE REACHES OUT HER HANDS TO THE POOR, AND EMBRACES THE NEEDY. SHE OPENS HER MOUTH IN WISDOM, AND ON HER TONGUE IS KINDLY COUNSEL. MANY ARE THE WOMEN OF PROVEN WORTH, BUT YOU HAVE EXCELLED THEM ALL.

PROVERBS 31: 20, 26, 29

THE TESTIMONY OF A SALVADORAN NUN

I DISCOVERED MY CALL

The following testimony was given by a Salvadoran nun working in a displaced persons camp. Like many religious men and women, she set out to "evangelize" the poor, only to discover that the poor evangelize us.

In my pastoral ministry I work with Christians and with those who say they are not Christians. Many of those who call themselves non-believers are more loving and closer to the Kingdom of God than are many of those who call themselves Christians.

Above all I have been impressed by the people's ability to forgive. They have suffered so much. Many were forced to abandon their homes and possessions. Many of their family members have been killed. But they have retained a great capacity to forgive, a difficult virtue. Sometimes a woman learns that her child was killed, and then in the Celebration of the Word, she prays from her heart for her enemies. She asks God to change their hearts and take away their blindness. Sometimes people are overcome by pain, but usually they are forgiving.

I want to share an example of how the displaced maintain their hope. One day, a woman who was in charge of distributing food told me she had had a problem:

"I was planning to help a woman I know, but her husband was killed by the death squads, and she fled to another village with her six children. Then another woman came to me, asking for the food that I was saving for my friend. She, too, was a widow with seven children. Her husband was a member of a death squad and for that he had been killed. I gave her the food I was saving for my friend."

The woman who told me this story is also a widow. Three of her children were killed by the death squads.

I was moved by this story. It shows how the poor, who have suffered most, understand the suffering of others. Their values are pure. The solidarity they give in the midst of their suffering is a sign that there will be reconciliation when peace comes to El Salvador. One day God will ask me and all of us what we have done for these people who cry out for help.

My experience has been similar to that of many other priests, nuns and laypeople. I have rediscovered my vocation. The poor have taught me the value of community life. Although they have faults, they share everything they have.

The contact with their poverty makes us feel ashamed of how we live, but it also challenges us to live more simply. When you see the courage and commitment of people who have to support families, it encourages us to live out our celibacy with greater willingness. The spirit of the Beatitudes and the Sermon on the Mount is present in the poor. In their prayers they do not ask God for vengeance, but for a change of heart in those who persecute them.

I believe this experience has been the greatest opportunity I have had to follow Jesus, to live out my vows, and to lead a more intense life of prayer among the poor. Some people tell me, "Be careful! Your vocation is in danger if you work with the displaced." But for me, and for many others, the poor give us the strength and determination to go forward.   *May 1982*

EACH ONE OF YOU HAS RECEIVED A SPECIAL GRACE, SO, LIKE GOOD STEWARDS, PUT IT AT THE SERVICE OF OTHERS.

I PETER 4: 10

| THE TESTIMONY OF A NORTH AMERICAN NUN

WHAT GIVES US HOPE

Sister Andrea Nenzel worked for more than two years in Calle Real, a displaced persons camp north of San Salvador. In 1987 she was elected provincial of her

religious community and had to return home. As the people gathered to say good-bye to Sister Andrea at a farewell Mass, they could hear Air Force planes bombing the nearby Guazapa volcano.

After the Mass, Sister Andrea shared the following reflection about her two years in the camp.

It is incredible how my life has been so closely identified with that of the displaced. I have spent 27 years as a pastoral worker, and have come to love many of the people I've worked with. But never before have I shared the lives of others so deeply, nor have others been so much a part of mine, as in this displaced persons camp.

If you look at the situation rationally, the normal tendency would be to despair, especially when everything you had—your family members, your home, your work—has been taken from you. Here I found exactly the opposite.

These people know God in a way I have never seen before. It is not uncommon to find people who are good, who pray, who know all about God, but it is rare to meet people who really know God, who consider God a friend, someone real in their lives who walks alongside them. What is truly exceptional is that the people as a community know God. They do not know a lot about theology. They would probably fail any catechetical exam. But they know God, and that is the source of their hope.

I remember one of the displaced, an 86-year-old man named Daniel, who was made deaf by the bombings. He suffered from chronic malaria and was close to death. Every day he prayed, and one of his prayers was that some day one of his children would find him, and that they would return home together.

That is just what happened. His daughter, who had been captured by the Army, later made her way to the camp. The two of them left for the village where they used to live. When I visited the village, Daniel looked younger than ever. He was working in the fields, tending the corn. He is the happiest man I have ever known.

The people, displaced by war, have begun to return to their homes in the war zones and have asked the Church to accompany them. Within our religious community we have reflected at length on the repopulation movement and our role of accompaniment. I can't say that I was not afraid; but the direction of my life is clear. We have to look at what gives us life and hope. I am convinced that if the people go back to their homes to rebuild, we should go with them.   *June 1987*

BEHOLD, I WILL BRING THEM BACK FROM THE LAND OF THE NORTH; I WILL GATHER THEM FROM THE ENDS OF THE WORLD, WITH THE BLIND AND THE LAME IN THEIR MIDST, THE MOTHERS AND THOSE WITH CHILD; THEY SHALL RETURN AS AN IMMENSE THRONG.
                              JEREMIAH 31:8

THOSE WHO HEAL THE WOUNDS OF WAR

The Salvadoran Army harasses international churchworkers, particularly those working in the repopulation sites, displaced persons camps and the war zones. During the November 1989 government crackdown, the security forces targeted international volunteers. More than forty religious and lay missionaries from the United States and other countries were captured or forced to leave. The following account was written in 1988.

Recently the military's campaign against international volunteers has intensified. The volunteer priests, nuns, pastors, teachers, doctors and nurses help those who suffer most the effects of the war. The international volunteers have been captured, detained and deported. There have also been official statements from the military High Command to humanitarian groups, and to the Catholic and Lutheran Churches, which make it clear that such a campaign is underway.

The military seeks to forbid or limit the presence and work of international volunteers in the country, especially in the war zones. The Army wants the Churches and international agencies to turn over lists of the names of their volunteers now working in such areas. The churchworkers have been subjected to increasingly harsh restrictions on their residency permits and on their work.

The Army justifies these restrictions by saying that the international churchworkers interfere with military operations against "terrorist delinquents." The Army claims that "terrorists" use civilians, including the internationals, for protection, for logistical support, and as a source of recruits. They claim that the safety of the volunteers is endangered in the war zones.

When international volunteers are not present, the poor, who suffer the most from the violent effects of the war, are the ones who are left without help, without consolation, and without protection.

The international volunteers do not impede military operations. Their only weapons are books, medicines and the Bible. Their goal is to be with the people in their suffering, to offer them hope, and to accompany them in the midst of the bombs and the bullets.

The real reason for the campaign against the international volunteers is that they are witnesses to the Army's violence against civilians. People are harassed, attacked, or "disappeared," and their food and possessions are stolen. When no international volunteers are present, it is much more dangerous to report these abuses. But when foreign volunteers describe what they have seen with their own eyes, the international community is alerted.

For the Salvadoran military, eyewitness reporting is a serious threat to their ability to act with impunity. Despite all the talk about "democratization," what the military fears most is the truth. So when these eyewitness testimonies come from North Americans, and the truth finds its way into the U.S. media, military officials are furious.

The Salvadoran government and the U.S. Embassy have not been terribly concerned about the welfare of the volunteers who do humanitarian work, but the government and the Embassy have welcomed those foreigners who come to El Salvador with millions of dollars and tons of bombs. It is ironic that you are welcome in El Salvador if you come to prolong the war, but if you come to work to heal the wounds of war, that is another matter entirely.

The poor do not consider the international volunteers as "foreigners," but as sisters and brothers. They have given the international volunteers the welcome they deserve, because the volunteers do not bring weapons, but rather they represent the best traditions of their countries.

February 1988

THIS IS WHAT WE PROCLAIM TO YOU: WHAT WAS FROM THE BEGINNING, WHAT WE HAVE HEARD, WHAT WE HAVE SEEN WITH OUR EYES, WHAT WE HAVE LOOKED UPON. WE PROCLAIM IT AND TURN TO YOU SO THAT YOU MAY SHARE LIFE WITH US.

I JOHN 1:1A,3A

ITA, MAURA, DOROTHY AND JEAN

On December 2, 1980 four North American churchwomen—three nuns and a lay missionary—were killed. Their bodies, exhumed from a shallow grave in the Department of La Libertad, showed signs of torture and rape. Despite intense international condemnation of the Salvadoran government, no military officer has been charged with this killing.

The U.S. is present in many ways in El Salvador. Military personnel and a fortress embassy, airplanes and bombs remind us of this every day. But we do not forget that solidarity and humanitarian aid also come to us from U.S. citizens. Many North Americans come here to inform themselves about our situation and return home to give testimony in their country. Others come to accompany our people. Some of them have remained forever.

Ita, Maura, Dorothy and Jean gave their lives for our people six years ago. Their names are joined forever to the names of Father Rutilio Grande, Archbishop Oscar Arnulfo Romero, Father Octavio Ortiz and countless other Salvadoran martyrs.

The Salvadoran people have not forgotten these four women. This year, on December 2, a Eucharist was again celebrated in their memory in the Cathedral to thank God for their commitment and generosity.

At the end of the Eucharist, some North Americans spoke. Ita's brother Bill, a well-known defender of the Salvadoran people, said that the death of his sister and her companions opened many people's eyes in the U.S., uniting the Salvadoran and the North American people with ties of blood.

He went on to say that it is tragic to think that the bullets and bombs which come from the United States are what have united Salvadorans and North Americans as brothers and sisters. But where sin abounds, grace abounds even more. Solidarity with El Salvador has grown since the killing of the four women. On this sixth anniversary, their martyrdom is being remembered throughout the United States, and many people are collecting funds for medical aid for the Salvadoran people.

Remembering the martyrs is a debt of gratitude, but even more, it is a sign that the Church in El Salvador is alive. Ten years have passed since the first priest was killed in El Salvador, but the light of the martyrs continues to shine.

The Mass in El Salvador is still unfinished. The sacrifice seems unending, and we long to celebrate the resurrection. The blood of the martyrs keeps our faith and Christian hope alive, encouraging us to continue working for justice and peace.
December 1986

EACH OF THE MARTYRS WAS GIVEN A LONG WHITE ROBE, AND THEY WERE TOLD TO BE PATIENT A LITTLE WHILE LONGER UNTIL THE QUOTA WAS FILLED WITH THEIR FELLOW SERVANTS AND SISTERS AND BROTHERS TO BE SLAIN, AS THEY HAD BEEN.

REVELATION 6:11

YOUR PEOPLE WILL BE MY PEOPLE

On December 2, 1988 the Conference of Religious Men and Women of El Salvador (CONFRES) celebrated a Eucharist in memory of the four North American church-women assassinated eight years ago. Monsignor Ricardo Urioste, Vicar of the Archdiocese of San Salvador, gave this homily.

Brothers and sisters, faith in the resurrection has called us together to remember our four sisters who were so cruelly murdered eight years ago. They gave their lives, lives that they had already given from the moment they arrived in this country. I believe that to give one's life consists above all in giving it every day, in every moment, in work, in selflessness, in being available to people.

In the first reading today, we heard the story of Ruth. Ruth, as we know, was a foreigner among the People of Israel. She was able to live fully the life of the poor. She became one with them. She said, "Your people will be my people, and your God will be my God. I will live with you until I am buried in your land."

St. Paul would later say, "There is among you neither Greek nor Jew for we are all one in Christ Jesus." This is how we want to see the Church, and this is how we saw these women.

One of the four women once wrote, "I know that we hardly make a difference, but if we can touch people with a little bit of love, even if it is just one or two people, that is already something great."

I think that all of us who work here, motivated as we are by our faith, want to serve the Lord, and we want to serve our sisters and brothers, especially the most defenseless, the most in need, the humblest and the poorest. The spirit of service comes from the poor. They teach us so much, and they evangelize us.

I am sure that you have experienced the same thing. I have become a different priest over these past dozen years. Before, I had not really discovered who our people are. I understand why the four women became enthusiastic when they discovered the richness of poverty. When you discover the strength of weakness, you, too, begin to feel stronger.

I think that each of you has experienced this teaching that the poor give us. They evangelize us, and they invite us with their life, their suffering, their pain, their tears and their blood to be the disciples that Jesus calls us to be.

On behalf of the Church, and especially the poor, I thank you for all you are doing. It's not important that your Spanish is not that good. I believe the poor feel very strong when you are present. It does not matter that sometimes you do not understand our way of life, like when we say "yes" and mean "no," or when we say, "We will do everything possible," and we don't do nearly as much as we could.

We are very indebted to these four women martyrs, and to all of you who have followed in their footsteps. I pray that the Lord will give a true, Christian meaning to our lives. Our inspiration is our faith in Jesus, our faith that he is our Saviour, and our faith that he gives us strength, encouragement and joy.

I am sure you feel great joy in working here. I personally would not be able to work in another country. That joy comes from Jesus to all of us who want to live the Gospel, to live our faith, and to live out this love in the way that he taught us. *December 1988*

BUT RUTH SAID, "DO NOT ASK ME TO ABANDON OR FORSAKE YOU! FOR WHEREVER YOU GO I WILL GO, WHEREVER YOU LODGE, I WILL LODGE, YOUR PEOPLE SHALL BE MY PEOPLE, AND YOUR GOD MY GOD. WHEREVER YOU DIE I WILL DIE, AND THERE BE BURIED."

RUTH 1:16-17A

AN EASTER HOMILY BY A SALVADORAN PRIEST

THE LAST WORD IS LIFE

Calavera, a village in the Department of Morazán, has suffered from the war for the last nine years. Its inhabitants have known every kind of repression: captures, killings, Army invasions, bombings. Their faith has been put to the test, but they remain steadfast.

On Saturday of Holy Week in 1989 the people gathered to celebrate the Easter Vigil. The following is the homily given by Father Miguel Ventura.

Dear brothers and sisters, we have the opportunity to gather at this time as we remember nine years of a cruel conflict. Many of us have felt, perhaps, that the light of a negotiated solution to the Salvadoran conflict has been snuffed out. Your presence here tonight, and your nine years of active participation in the construction of this new society, is the clearest expression of the resurrected Christ.

A few days ago, I visited the village of Junquillo, near the Torola River. That community suffered a terrible bombing attack on March 8. A bomb fell two yards from one of the houses, destroying it completely. Five people died and five others were seriously injured.

I arrived in the community four days after the bombing and met the family members of the victims. I saw the pain in the eyes of the father. Three of his children had been killed and three others injured. None of us could have been there without feeling his anguish. We can all understand the pain of that father.

But in the midst of that pain and in the midst of a home which was completely destroyed, we saw another aspect of suffering. The community had gathered to share in the family's grief. One of those present said to me, "In our community, all of us have been touched by this tragedy. All of us carry this cross and we can rise above the suffering."

I believe there are no wiser words than these. They showed me in a powerful way that as a community, we can overcome all the barriers that separate us from each other and confront any trial.

What does Christ say to a people at war who have suffered 70,000 dead, more than a million refugees and displaced people, 7,000 disappeared, and thousands of prisoners? What purpose does the blood of Monsignor Romero and of Father Octavio Ortiz serve when we see a right-wing power emerge at this time? What do the events of almost 2,000 years ago have to say to us?

In the time of Jesus, his followers asked the same questions: Who has the last word in history? Will it be the Roman Empire? Will it be the oppressive powers that condemn the poor? Will it be death or life?

On this night of resurrection, we must understand that we are not walking toward death, but advancing day by day toward life. Christ seems defeated but rises again on the third day. His enemies place guards around his tomb. But Christ rises up victoriously and says with a loud voice: "The God of life has the last word!"

Brothers and sisters, you who have wandered these hills; you who have left loved ones along the way; you whose children have died and watered this soil with their blood; you whose family members have been imprisoned and tortured; I ask you: Who has the last word in history? At this difficult time, remember: the idols of power and money do not have the final word.

You, brothers and sisters, are the living testimony that Christ is the last word, that your profound faith is the last word. We are gathered as a People of God, as a church of pilgrims, in the midst of this martyrdom, proclaiming that the God of history and the God of resurrection has the last word! *April 1989*

THEN I SAW A NEW HEAVEN AND A NEW EARTH... I HEARD A LOUD VOICE FROM THE THRONE CRY OUT: "GOD SHALL BE FOR THIS PEOPLE AND THIS PEOPLE SHALL BE OF GOD. GOD SHALL WIPE AWAY EVERY TEAR FROM THEIR EYES AND THERE SHALL BE NO MORE DEATH OR MOURNING, CRYING OUT OR PAIN, FOR THE FORMER WORLD HAS PASSED AWAY."
REVELATION 21:1A,3,4

On this night of Resurrection, we must understand that we are not walking toward death, but advancing day by day toward life.

THIS, TOO, THE ANGEL SAID TO ME, "DO NOT KEEP THE PROPHE-
CIES IN THIS BOOK A SECRET, BECAUSE TIME IS CLOSE... LOOK, I
AM COMING SOON AND MY REWARD IS WITH ME, TO REPAY EVERY-
ONE AS THEIR DEEDS DESERVE. I AM THE ALPHA AND THE OMEGA,
THE FIRST AND THE LAST, THE BEGINNING AND THE END. BLESSED
ARE THOSE WHO WILL HAVE WASHED THEIR ROBES CLEAN, SO THAT
THEY WILL HAVE THE RIGHT TO FEED ON THE TREE OF LIFE."

REVELATION 22

RECOMMENDED READING

One Day of Life, by Manlio Argueta. Random House. (A novel)

The Religious Roots of Rebellion: Christians in Central American Revolutions, by Philip Berryman. Orbis Books.

Salvador Witness: The Life and Calling of Jean Donovan, by Ana Carrigan. Ballantine.

War Against the Poor: Low Intensity Conflict and the Christian Faith, by Jack Nelson-Pallmeyer. Orbis Books.

The Promised Land: Peasant Revolution in Chalatenango, by Jenny Pearce. Monthly Review.